★ ★ ★ KID ★ ★ ★ INNOVATORS

TRUE TALES OF CHILDHOOD FROM

INVENTORS AND TRAILBLAZERS

STORIES BY *ROBIN STEVENSON*   ILLUSTRATIONS BY *ALLISON STEINFELD*

WALT DISNEY

RESHMA SAUJANI

STEVE JOBS

FLORENCE NIGHTINGALE

 * * * # KID * * *
INNOVATORS

TRUE TALES OF CHILDHOOD FROM
INVENTORS AND TRAILBLAZERS

STORIES BY *ROBIN STEVENSON* ILLUSTRATIONS BY *ALLISON STEINFELD*

JACQUES COUSTEAU

MADAM CJ WALKER

ALAN TURING

ALVIN AILEY

Library of Congress Cataloging in Publication Data
Stevenson, Robin, 1968- author. | Steinfeld, Allison, illustrator.
Kid innovators : true tales of childhood from inventors and trailblazers / stories by Robin Stevenson ; illustrations by Allison Steinfeld.
Biographies of Grace Hopper, Steve Jobs, Bill Gates, Reshma Saujani and twelve others.
LCSH: Inventors—Biography—Juvenile literature. | Businesspeople—Biography—Juvenile literature.
LCC T39 .S95 2021 | DDC 309.2/53—dc23
2020039476

ISBN: 978-1-68369-227-0

Printed in China

Typeset in Bulmer MT, Bell MT, Linowrite, and Bulldog

Designed by Andie Reid
Illustrations by Allison Steinfeld
Production management by John J. McGurk

Quirk Books
215 Church Street
Philadelphia, PA 19106
quirkbooks.com

10 9 8 7 6 5 4 3 2 1

*To my own kid innovator, Kai, for making
me see the world differently; and to David,
Genevieve and Quentin. So much love to you all.*

Table of Contents

PART 3

Cracking Codes and Saving Lives

PART 4

Trailblazers

Introduction

Do you sometimes think differently than the people around you? Do you like to do things your own way? Do you ever dream of inventing something new, or finding a solution for a big problem?

If so, then maybe you will become an innovator! Innovators are trailblazers. They think outside the box, tackle tough challenges, pursue their passions, and chase their dreams—and in the process, they change our world.

Some innovators are inventors: they tinker, experiment, and design new things. Others combine inventions that already exist or use current technology in original ways. Some innovators are entrepreneurs, bringing new products to millions of people around the world. And some transform and revolutionize the fields they work in by challenging old ways of doing things or approaching problems in a different way.

The innovators in this book started out as inquisitive kids. They were full of questions and hungry for knowledge. Grace Hopper was so curious about how alarm clocks worked that she took apart all seven of the ones in her home. Most of these innovators read voraciously as children: Elon Musk and Bill Gates both read encyclopedias from A to Z!

Many of the things we take for granted in our daily lives exist because of innovators. But people don't always welcome change, and innovation is often met with skepticism and even scorn. Experts predicted that cell phones would never replace wired phones. The idea that we might send objects into space was considered to be absurd. And flight was seen as preposterous: "Heavier-than-air flying machines are impossible," one famous scientist stated confidently—only eight years before the Wright brothers achieved their first flight.

Woohoo!!!

Innovators are people who make the impossible possible. To do that, they need the confidence and strength to go against the crowd. They need to be persistent, and they can't afford to worry too much about what people think. So, it is not surprising that innovators often started out as strong-willed and independent-minded children—which wasn't always easy for their parents and teachers! When Elon Musk was six, his mom said that he was grounded, so he walked the ten miles across town to a birthday party. Steve Jobs was a troublemaker who played tricks on his classmates and was sent home from school repeatedly. And Florence Nightingale liked to question everything—much to the despair of her mother, who thought she should be more obedient.

Although they were very intelligent, these innovators did not always do well in school. Many were messy, disorganized, or absent-minded; others wanted to work only on the subjects that interested them. Quite a few of them had little in common with other kids their age and cared more about their own ideas than anything else: Jacques Cousteau was a loner, Alan

Turing was a daydreamer, and Bill Gates wanted to stay in his room reading all day.

These innovators all started out as little kids with big ideas—and although they often faced obstacles and challenges, they grew up to be adults who pursued their interests with great creativity and passion. Without the innovators in this book, our world would be a very different place. May their stories inspire you to follow your own dreams and blaze your own trail!

PART

ONE

TECH
REVOLUTION

FROM THE FIRST

PROGRAMMING LANGUAGE

* * TO THE * *

CELL PHONES

IN OUR POCKETS,

THESE

KID INNOVATORS

HELPED MAKE

COMPUTER TECHNOLOGY

a part of our

EVERYDAY LIVES.

GRACE HOPPER

> The Grand Lady
> of Software

Grace Hopper is famous for her work in the development of COBOL, one of the first computer programming languages. In fact, she is sometimes referred to as the grandmother of COBOL or the Grand Lady of Software. But when she was young, she didn't dream of working with computers—because there were no computers to work with!

Grace was born in 1906, at her grandparents' home in New York City. Her parents, Walter Fletcher Murray and Mary Campbell Van Horne, were a wealthy couple, and she was their first child. They named her after Mary's best friend. Soon after Grace was born, she and her parents moved into a trendy new apartment building near Manhattan's Soldiers' and Sailors' Monument. Three years later, her sister Mary was born, followed by her brother Roger.

One of Grace's earliest memories was of meeting her great-grandfather, a retired navy admiral, when she was only two. She remembered him as a large man with a silver-topped cane and white mutton-chop whiskers. Although he died when Grace was young, this encounter helped spark her own interest in the navy.

Grace's childhood was happy and secure. Her father was an insurance broker, and her mother loved math, puzzles, and games of all kinds. Grace grew up in a house full of books, with parents who supported her learning and encouraged her curiosity. She was born with a strong desire to figure out how things worked. When she was seven, she decided to take apart her alarm clock, but when she unscrewed the back cover, all the springs, cogs, and gears came tumbling out before she could get a good look at the mechanism. Grace then proceeded to take apart every alarm clock in the house—seven in total. Her mother did not want to discourage her inquisitiveness and experimentation, but she asked Grace to please stick to one clock only from then on!

Soon after this incident, Grace's father developed a medical problem that required both of his legs to be amputated at the knee. In those days, few women drove, but Grace's mother immediately went out and bought a Model-T Ford. On the weekends, she drove her children to various activities, and when her husband was well enough, she drove him to work every day.

Luckily, Grace's dad recovered well. His business prospered, and he returned to his hobby of golfing. With prosthetic legs and two canes, he was able to get around, and he used thumbtacks to stick his socks to his wooden legs. He used to joke with his kids that he didn't need to change his socks as often as they did— only when they got dusty, he said!

In the early 1900s, girls were not given much education. In most wealthy middle-class families, girls were not expected to ever work outside the home; it was assumed that they would marry and have children. But Grace's parents were unusual: they wanted their daughters to be well-educated. Her dad, worried about his own health, thought they should be able to support themselves in case something happened to him. Grace's mother, like Grace herself, was highly intelligent and opinionated. She was interested in politics and enjoyed discussing her views, which were often strong ones! She did not have the opportunity to go to college, but she was determined that her own daughters would.

As the oldest child in her family, Grace had the most responsibilities; her sister Mary later said that she and Roger had fun together, but that Grace was "kind of a bore!" It was often up to Grace to tell her younger siblings what to do, and they didn't always appreciate it. But the three of them had plenty of adventures together, playing in Riverside Park or spending weekends at their paternal grandparents' home in Plainfield, New Jersey. Their maternal grandparents still lived in the city, and they often visited them as well. Mary took her children to concerts, lectures, historic sites, and museums; they visited every museum in New York City, Grace later said.

Grace attended the Graham School, one of the oldest girls' schools in New York City, but much of her learning happened at home. She read voraciously; books were always what she asked for at Christmas. Her parents encouraged her and her siblings to think for themselves, to come up with original ideas, and to be able to defend their views. Both Walter and Mary enjoyed debating, and they expected the kids to take part. Grace learned how to argue a point logically and back it up with evidence. She was quiet but confident, focused, and direct—and she could be very persuasive. When she was ten, she wrote in the school yearbook:

Charlotte Herbig

Spanish Club and the Debate Team.

Grace Hopper

Faithfulness in all things
My motto is you see;
The world will be a better place
When all agree with me.

Hea
act

Faithfulness in all things
My motto is you see;
The world will be a better place
When all agree with me.

Summers were a special time for Grace and her extended family. From the time Grace was a baby, they spent the summers in New Hampshire, along with her aunts and uncles and more than thirty cousins. The families owned most of the property on one edge of a lake. It was a two-day trip for Grace and her family to reach the site. They would take a night boat out of New York City, then a train, a trolley, and another train, followed by a final little railway around the north side of the lake.

All summer long, the kids swam and sailed and canoed and hiked; they grew vegetables and learned to cook and sew. These were all things that Grace's mother saw as essential life skills. Grace learned needlepoint, knitting and crocheting, and playing piano. The kids called their summer homes "camps," and they called Grace's parents the Warden (that was Walter) and the Chief Warden (that was Mary). Grace's mother posted house rules, such as asking permission before going out in the canoes, but the kids had a lot of freedom and were encouraged to be independent and resourceful.

Grace's dad had a workshop in an old boathouse at the lake, where he liked to make things out of wood—everything from cabinets to little model houses for the kids. Grace inherited his love of tools and tinkering, and she spent many hours building things from a construction kit. And, of course, she spent a lot of time sitting on the front steps, lost in a good book. All her life, she had fond memories of those long summer months spent in nature.

When Grace was seventeen, she took a Latin entrance exam for Vassar College but failed. Instead, she went to the Partridge School in Plainfield, New Jersey, and studied hard, preparing to try again. She enjoyed her time at the school, staying there during the week and returning home on weekends. A year later, she was accepted at Vassar and began her college education. At that time, girls were encouraged to take courses called "Husband and Wife" and "Motherhood." Unemployment rates were high, and many people saw working women as taking jobs away from men. Most of Grace's classmates had no goals other than to get married. But Grace ignored these pressures and studied physics and mathematics, graduating with honors and going on to earn the highest academic degree: a PhD.

When World War II began, the navy was reluctant to admit women, but Grace was keen to sign up. She thought she could contribute more by working for the navy than she could by teaching mathematics. At first, navy officials wouldn't accept her—she was too thin, they said—but eventually she convinced them that she was healthy. The navy needed someone with her mathematical skills, so Grace was sent to Harvard University, where she was directed to a room in the basement and shown a huge, noisy machine. "That's a computing engine," her boss told her. He handed her a codebook and gave her a week to learn how to program.

The computer was the Harvard Mark 1, and Grace was one of its first programmers. After the war ended in 1945, Grace joined the Eckert-Mauchy Computer Corporation and was part of the team that developed the UNIVAC 1 computer. She believed that it would be much easier for people to write programs using English words rather than symbols. Lots of people thought that was impossible because, they said, computers don't understand English. So Grace created the first "compiler": a program that allowed computers to translate English words into code. Soon, she was leading the department and developing some of the first compiler-based programming languages—FLOW-

MATIC and MATH-MATIC. This work laid the foundation for Common Business-Oriented Language, or COBOL, which quickly became the most popular language in the business community.

Throughout her life, Grace Hopper had strong views and boundless energy, and she believed in innovation above all. She wanted people to avoid being tied to old ways of doing things. She was also a firm believer in encouraging young people to take risks and pursue their passions. "Teach them to go ahead and do it," she said. "Teach them to have courage. Teach them to use their intuition, to stick their necks out. I always tell young people: Go ahead and do it. You can always apologize later."

A hundred years before Grace Hopper's ground-breaking work, **Ada Lovelace** defied convention by becoming not only a mathematician but also the world's first computer programmer. As a child, though, Ada wanted to fly. She researched birds and ways of designing wings, recording her findings in a guide that she called "Flyology." Ada's mother encouraged her to abandon her creative project and return to her math studies. It was highly unusual for a girl in the early 1800s to be educated in math, but Ada had an unusual mother as well as a remarkable talent. When she was seventeen years old, she met the famous mathematician and inventor Charles Babbage, who told her about a machine he had designed. Ada quickly grasped not only how the machine worked but its incredible potential as well. She explained how it might perform a calculation, and she wrote a detailed plan that is now considered to be the world's first computer program.

STEVE JOBS

Love
What
You Do

Steve Jobs is best known for Mac computers, iPhones, and iPads, but his innovative ideas also transformed the music, movie, and digital-publishing industries. As an adult, he was both brilliant and difficult. Even as a small child, he wanted to do things his own way.

Steve was born in San Francisco, on February 24, 1955. His birth parents were a graduate student named Joanna Schieble and a Syrian teaching assistant named Abdulfattah Jandali. Joanne and Abdullah had met at the University of Wisconsin, fallen in love, and traveled to Syria together. When Joanne became pregnant, they were not ready to become parents. Once back home, they decided to place their baby for adoption.

Paul and Clara Jobs had been wanting a child for many years before one finally came into their lives. They adopted Joanne and Abdullah's son and named him Steven Paul. Steve grew into an active and curious toddler. Twice they had to rush him to the emergency room: one time because Steve had stuck a metal pin into an electric socket and burned his hand, and another time because he had eaten poison!

28

When Steve was two, his parents adopted a baby girl named Patty. Three years later, the family moved to the town of Mountain View, near Palo Alto, in California. Steve later said that his childhood home was one of the things that inspired him as a designer. "We had nice toasty floors when I was a kid," he said, remembering the radiant heating in the house. "I love it when you can bring really great design and simple capability to something that doesn't cost much."

Steve always knew he was adopted. When he was about six years old, he told a little girl who lived across the street. "So, does that mean your real parents didn't want you?" she asked. Steve ran home crying. His parents explained that was not the case at all. "We specifically picked you," they said, speaking with great emphasis to make sure he understood. "I've always felt special," Steve later said. "My parents made me feel special."

The family's house had a garage where Paul, a mechanic, could work on his cars. He marked off one section of a table and told Steve, "This is your workbench now." Steve wasn't interested in cars, but he liked spending time tinkering with his dad. When Paul went to the junkyard to look for parts, Steve went along. He admired his dad's attention to detail. "He loved doing things right," Steve said. "He even cared

about the look of the parts you couldn't see."

Growing up in Silicon Valley, Steve had many neighbors who worked as engineers. One of them, Larry Lang, became an important mentor. "What Larry did to get to know the kids in the block was rather a strange thing," Steve explained. "He put out a carbon microphone and a battery and a speaker on his driveway where you could talk into the microphone and your voice would be amplified by the speaker."

Steve's father had told him that an electronic amplifier was needed to do this, but here was a system that worked without one. "I proudly went home to my father and announced that he was all wrong and that this man up the block was amplifying voice with just a battery," he recalled. "My father told me that I didn't know what I was talking about and we got into a very large argument." So, Steve dragged his dad to Larry's house so he could see it for himself.

Over the next few years, Larry taught Steve a lot about electronics. He introduced him to Heathkits, a type of kit with detailed instructions for making items like television receivers and radio equipment. Steve said that these kits not only taught him how things worked but also helped him develop a belief that even things that seemed complex—like televisions and radios—could be studied and understood.

Steve's mom, Clara, taught him to read before he started kindergarten. In the classroom, though, Steve's learning did not go smoothly. His first school was Monta Loma Elementary, just four blocks from his house. "I was kind of bored for the first few years, so I occupied myself by getting into trouble," he admitted.

Steve's best friend was a boy named Rick. One time, he and Rick made posters advertising "Bring Your Pet to School Day." Kids showed up with their animals and chaos broke loose, with dogs chasing cats all over the school. Another time, Steve and Rick persuaded the other students to tell them their bike lock combinations. Once they knew dozens of combinations, they undid the locks and switched them around. When school ended that day, the students couldn't unlock their bikes. According to Steve, it took until ten o'clock that night to sort out the mess.

Another time, Steve let a snake loose in the classroom, and then he set off a small explosion under the teacher's chair. By the end of third grade, Steve had been sent home from school several times. His parents didn't punish him, though. They thought it was partly the school's fault—Steve was misbehaving because he wasn't being challenged in class. Steve agreed, saying that he was always being asked to "memorize stupid stuff."

But being bored was only part of the problem. Steve also had a strong dislike for authority and hated being told what to do. Luckily, in fourth grade, he had a teacher who understood him. Mrs. Hill started out by bribing Steve to do math problems, but before long, he was enjoying learning and wanted to please her. "I learned more from her than any other teacher," Steve said. If it hadn't been for Mrs. Hill, he admitted, "I'm sure I would've gone to jail."

Mrs. Hill recognized that Steve needed to be challenged, and the school recommended that he skip two grades. His parents thought that was too much, but they agreed to let Steve move up from fourth grade to sixth. That meant switching to another school.

At Crittenden Middle School, the environment was much rougher, and fights were common. Being a year younger than the other students was hard, and Steve was often bullied. His sixth-grade report card noted that he had trouble getting motivated. Halfway through seventh grade, Steve decided he'd had enough. "He came home one day," recalled his father, "and said if he had to go back there again, he just wouldn't go." His parents decided to move to an area with better schools. They scraped together the money and bought a home in Los Altos, a few miles away.

In ninth grade, Steve started at Homestead High. The school had an electronics class with a well-equipped lab and a passionate teacher named Mr. McCollum. But Steve, with his rebellious attitude and rejection of authority, clashed with the teacher. According to Mr. McCollum, Steve was usually "off in a corner doing something on his own and really didn't want to have much of anything to do with either me or the rest of the class." Although he loved electronics, Steve dropped the course.

Outside school, however, Steve was beginning to find others who shared his interests. He joined the Explorer's Club at Hewlett-Packard, where Larry Lang worked. The students met in the cafeteria, where engineers would talk to them about their projects: lasers, holography, light-emitting diodes. Steve was in heaven. It was at HP that he saw his first computer. "I fell in love with it," he said.

Steve was also working on a project of his own: he wanted to build a frequency counter to measure the rate of pulses in an electronic signal. He didn't have all the parts he needed, so he looked in the phone book for Bill Hewlett, the head of Hewlett-Packard, and called him at home. Not only did he get the parts he needed, but Bill

also gave him a summer job in a factory that made frequency counters.

It was while he was still in high school that Steve Jobs met his future business partner, Steve Wozniak. Wozniak was five years older and highly adept with electronics. In fact, he had learned some of his skills in Mr. McCollum's class. When Steve was twenty-one, he and Wozniak founded the Apple Computer Company. At first, they worked out of Steve's bedroom, and later they moved the business into the Jobs family's garage. Two years later, Steve had earned more than a million dollars—and by the time he was twenty-five, he'd made over 250 million dollars.

Many of the things we use in our daily lives wouldn't exist if it weren't for Steve Jobs: Mac computers, iPhones, iPods and iPads, iTunes, Apple Stores, even Pixar's *Toy Story*! But money wasn't what drove him. "You've got to find what you love," he said. "Your work is going to fill a large part of your life, and the only way to be truly satisfied is to do what you believe is great work. And the only way to do great work is to love what you do. If you haven't found it yet, keep looking."

BILL GATES

I'm
Thinking!

Bill Gates is an American software
developer and entrepreneur, famous for
cofounding the technology company Microsoft.
But his interest in innovation extends beyond
computers. He is also working to find creative
ways to solve global problems and reduce
inequality around the world.

Bill was born in Seattle on October 28, 1955. His father, William (who was called Bill Senior), was a lawyer, and his mother, Mary, was a former schoolteacher who worked for nonprofit organizations. She was the first woman to hold several leadership positions with the United Way.

Bill was an energetic baby and was always smiling. His parents gave him the nickname Happy Boy. He liked rocking in his cradle and, when he got a little older, on a rocking horse. (As an adult, Bill still likes to rock. He says it helps him think.) Bill's sister, Kristianne, is two years older, and they enjoyed playing make-believe games together. According to Kristi, Bill would always pretend to be the dog!

Because their parents were busy working, Bill's grandmother looked after him and Kristi after school.

They called her Gam. She taught them to play cards and gave Bill the nickname Trey, which is a bridge term. It was less confusing than calling both him and his dad by the same name.

The whole family loved games. When Bill and Kristi were nine and ten years old, their parents invited them to play hangman. Once the kids deciphered the words, they read a surprising message: "A little visitor is coming soon." It was their parents' way of telling them that a baby was on the way. Their new sister was named Libby.

Bill read constantly. By age nine, he had gone through all the entries in the *World Book Encyclopedia* from A to Z! When his teachers held summer reading contests to see who could read the most books over the holidays, Bill wanted to win—and he did.

But despite his love of reading, Bill didn't do well in elementary school. He got As in math, but Cs and Ds in handwriting and other subjects. He was left-handed, but when he was bored he would try to write with his right hand, just for the added challenge. To the frustration of his teachers, he would often goof around or argue. He loved the school library, though, and spent hours tracking down missing books. If his teachers didn't encourage him to go outside and play, he would work right through recess.

Summers were good times for Bill. The Gates family and their friends rented cabins on the Hood Canal, where they water-skied and had picnics and campfires. They called it Camp Cheerio, and Bill's dad was the mayor. The kids played ball games, ran obstacle courses, and had three-legged races in what they called the Cheerio Olympics. "At Cheerio, getting your spot on the podium was really important," his sister Libby said.

Bill also enjoyed Boy Scouts. He hiked and camped, earning merit badges for woodworking, basket weaving, and swimming. He also held an unofficial record for being the dirtiest Boy Scout, perhaps because he would go hiking in white T-shirts and shorts!

From the time he was young, Bill was strong-willed and independent. He recalls, "My parent's authority seemed arbitrary. I really didn't want to follow their

rules." By age eleven, his relationship with his mother was difficult. One evening at dinner, Bill shouted at her. His dad was so upset that he threw a glass of water at Bill.

Realizing something needed to change, Bill's family went to see a counselor. Bill explained that he was at war with his parents. The counselor pointed out that it wasn't a fair war because he was hurting his parents—and they were really on his side! Bill later said that the counselor was a cool guy who taught him a lot about psychology. He helped Bill see that he didn't always need to fight, and he helped Bill's parents accept their son's need for more freedom.

As a kid, Libby sometimes thought Bill was strange. Their sister Kristi agreed. "I think that, left to his own devices, he might have stayed in his room and read books all day long," she said. "You could just see that he was different. Bill just wanted to sit in his room—reading, thinking, chewing on pencils." When his parents asked what he was doing behind his closed bedroom door, he would reply: "I'm thinking!"

Bill's parents were worried about how their son would cope in middle school. He was small and disorganized, and he had little in common with kids his age. They decided to send him to Lakeside School, a private boys' school. Students at Lakeside wore uniforms and carried briefcases, and Bill wasn't sure he wanted to go. He liked to goof around and make people laugh. What if this new school was too strict? He considered deliberately doing badly on the entrance exam so that he wouldn't get in—but when the time came, he couldn't bring himself to do less than his best work.

At Lakeside, Bill found something that would change his life: a bulky machine with a keyboard and a roll of paper. It was an ASR-33 teletype. It had a modem that connected it through the telephone line to a mainframe computer at the General Electric office. In the days before the invention of personal computers (PCs), these mainframe computers were enormous, at least the size of a refrigerator, and cost millions of dollars. Most organizations couldn't afford them—and schools certainly were unable to buy them. So, instead, the school bought computer time on General Electric's mainframe.

Another Lakeside student, Paul Allen, heard that Bill had done exceptionally well on a nationwide math test, so he invited Bill to join the Lakeside Programmers Group. Paul was older and wore a black leather jacket, and Bill thought he was extremely cool. The teachers didn't know much about computers, so the students and adults taught themselves from computer manuals. Paul taught Bill a lot about coding. At age thirteen, Bill wrote his first computer program, making a tic-tac-toe game.

Bill spent so much time in the computer room that other students complained he was monopolizing the equipment. Luckily, a group from the University of Washington Computer Center came to the rescue. They had started a private organization called Computer Center Corporation, or C-Cubed, and installed a state-of-the-art computer in a former automobile showroom. They were planning to sell computer time to businesses and engineering firms, but first they needed to make sure everything was working properly. C-Cubed's founder had a son at Lakeside, and she suggested hiring the students to test the new computer's software. They would be paid with free computer time. Bill was in heaven.

Bill was so fanatical about the computer that he ignored everything else. His room was messier than ever. His mom started picking up the clothes he left on the floor and charging him to get them back, but it didn't work—Bill didn't care what he wore. So, his parents started keeping the door to his room shut, which Bill appreciated because then he could sneak out and go to C-Cubed! Sometimes, he would stay so late that the buses stopped running and he had to walk home. When his mom found out, she finally understood why he had so much trouble getting up in the mornings.

In eighth grade, Bill became best friends with a student named Kent Evans. The two boys hung out at each other's houses, and they spent what Bill called "ridiculous amounts" of time on the phone. Bill and Kent were the youngest kids in the Programmers Group, and when a local company hired the group to program their payroll, the high school students didn't want the two middle schoolers involved.

Bill told the older students: "I think you're underestimating how hard this is. If you ask me to come back, I am going to be totally in charge." Sure enough they did, and Bill took over. "It was just more natural for me to be in charge," he said.

Bill and Kent often talked about the future and what they would do in the world. When they were in tenth grade, a Lakeside teacher recruited them to help write a program to manage the school's class scheduling system. It was a very challenging project. They worked day and night, even sleeping in the computer lab, hoping to finish before school started.

Then, something terrible happened. Kent took a weekend off to go mountain climbing and he slipped and fell to his death. It was a huge loss. Bill decided that he would still do the things he and Kent had talked about, even though he would have to do them without his friend. He was determined to finish their scheduling project. Paul Allen stepped in to help, and they got it done just in time.

When Bill was nearly seventeen, he and Paul started their first business together. It was called Traf-O-Data, and its goal was to find a faster, cheaper way of analyzing the information collected in traffic surveys.

Although the business didn't lead to the riches Bill had hoped for, he and Paul learned a great deal about microprocessors, which helped pave the way for their future success.

Bill graduated from high school and went on to study at Harvard University, but after two years of college, he dropped out to start another company with Paul. He was nineteen, and that company would become Microsoft. Today, Bill Gates is one of the richest people in the world. He and his wife, Melinda, used the wealth generated by Microsoft to create the Bill and Melinda Gates Foundation. Through their donations, they tackle social problems such as unsafe drinking water, diseases, hunger, and climate change to improve people's lives and make our world a better and more equal place.

RESHMA SAUJANI

Embracing
Failure

Reshma Saujani is an American lawyer and politician, but she is best known as the founder of Girls Who Code, an international nonprofit organization that teaches girls computer coding. Along the way, it encourages them to be brave, take risks, and support one another.

Reshma's parents arrived in the United States as refugees from Uganda, a country in East Africa. Her father, Mukund, and her mother, Meena, were among the 80,000 people of South Asian heritage who lived there. Many were the descendants of workers who went to Uganda from India during the late 1800s, when Uganda was a British colony. They now owned shops and factories, and their businesses were a crucial part of the Ugandan economy. Mukund's and Meena's family had lived in Uganda for two generations, and they both worked as engineers.

Then, in 1971, a dictator named Idi Amin took control of the country. He blamed Ugandan Asians for taking jobs. He stole their businesses and property and ordered them to leave the country immediately. Mukund and Meena had to search for a place that

would let them in. Luckily, the United States responded to their plea and granted them refugee status, which likely saved their lives.

They resettled in Schaumberg, a medium-sized Midwest town near Chicago, Illinois. "My father always tells the story that they took out a map of the United States, got a dart, threw it and [Chicago is] where it landed," Reshma says. A few months later, their first daughter, Keshma was born, and in 1975, Reshma came along.

Life wasn't easy for the family. They lived in an area of mostly white families, and they faced prejudice and racism. "My father had to change his name from Mukund to Mike just to get a job," Reshma recalled. People even threw eggs and toilet paper at their home.

Mukund and Meena spoke little English, and they couldn't find work as engineers. Meena took a job selling cosmetics, and Mukund found work as a machinist. They had to work very hard, and their jobs paid a lot less than engineering. "My parents worked all the time," Reshma recalled. "In the morning, we woke up, we were dropped off at a babysitter before school who lived across the street from our school. My parents were busy and they were working to put food on the table, so we didn't have all these activities after school. We went to school, then we came home and made ourselves a snack and put on the TV and waited until our parents came home for dinner."

It was the lack of family and community that was hardest for Reshma's parents. They placed a great deal of importance on education and community involvement. Even though he was busy and tired, Reshma's father often took his daughters to the library and always read books to them. In Uganda, he explained, the Indian community had not been much involved in politics; as a result of what had happened there, he felt that political awareness was vital. He read Reshma biographies of activists like Martin Luther King Jr., Eleanor Roosevelt, and Mahatma Gandhi— people who had seen injustice and stepped up to fight it.

As a young child, Reshma decided she wanted to make a difference and get involved in politics. She was twelve years old when she saw a movie about a fearless lawyer, and she decided to pursue law. She used to tape lists of the top-ranked law schools on the refrigerator; soon, she knew where she wanted to go. "I decided I wanted to go to Yale Law school . . . because it was the best," she said. "I was definitely a motivated, ambitious kid."

The day before Reshma's eighth-grade graduation, a group of schoolgirls beat her up, leaving her with a black eye. "Racism was rampant," she said. "I can't count the number of times I was asked whether my mother was born with a dot on her head." Reshma was called names and teased about the color of her skin. She wanted to fight back—but not physically. For one thing, she felt that her small size was, in her own words, "hardly an intimidating presence." Reshma needed to come up with another strategy to advocate for change.

Upon starting high school that fall, Reshma asked a teacher if she could launch a student organization. She called it PRISM: Prejudice Reduction Interested Students Movement. As one of the few Indian girls at her school, she wanted to help her peers learn about her own and other cultures. Fifty students joined, and the group sponsored a cultural show at the end of the school year. The group still exists, although it is now called the Diversity Club. Reshma was learning how much people can accomplish when they work together, and she was discovering "the thrilling power of building a movement to effect change." It was the first time she founded an organization, but it wouldn't be the last.

Reshma's father always pushed her to work hard and do her best. "When I won an award or got a top grade, my father never applauded me," she said. "When I stumbled, he never told me it was okay." As a result, Reshma developed a high tolerance for criticism—a useful trait for someone who wants to go into politics. Her father's approach to failure taught her an important lesson, she said. "We have to get up when we fall, learn from our mistakes, and try to do better the next time."

After high school, Reshma decided to study political science, and she continued her activism for diversity on campus. Afterward, she moved to Washington, D.C. to work as an intern at the White House. "I'm the daughter of refugees," she said. "The immigrant mentality is to work hard, be brave, and never give up in your pursuit of achieving the American dream." When Reshma applied to Yale Law School, she was rejected three times, but she didn't give up. Finally, she was accepted.

But after becoming a lawyer and working in New York's Financial District, Reshma wasn't happy. She decided that she wanted to pursue her old passion for politics and public service. She wanted to make a difference. So, she ran for Congress—but lost.

Reshma was devastated, but she found a way to embrace and learn from this failure. "Being brave, regardless of the outcome, is what ultimately led me to start Girls Who Code," she said. When she was running for office, she had seen the huge inequality in the education system; some schools had high-tech robotics labs, while others had just one old computer in the basement. She noticed something else, too. "Why are there all boys in the computer science classrooms? Why are there all boys on the robotics team?" she wondered. It was clear that the technology field still had a big gender gap—and she decided to do something about it.

In 2012, she offered the first Girls Who Code class in New York City. Twenty teen girls, most from high schools with few resources, came to learn Python and write their own computer programs. Many of them went on to start coding clubs at their schools, and Girls Who Code began to grow! It now has school clubs and summer programs in all fifty states and in Canada, and more than 185,000 girls have taken part in its programs. "Coding is the language of the future, and every girl should learn it," Reshma says.

Drawing on her own experience, Reshma Saujani encourages girls to embrace failure as part of learning: "If you haven't failed, you haven't done enough yet," she said. "I think failure is so important because it teaches you bravery, and it also leads you to a more authentic life."

We tend to hear a lot about U.S. inventors and entrepreneurs, but innovation in computing has happened all around the world. The first computer was invented by the British mathematician **Charles Babbage** in the mid-1800s. Before that, a "computer" was a person—someone whose job was adding and subtracting numbers and writing down the results. Another British computer scientist, Sir Tim Berners-Lee, invented the World Wide Web in 1989. And two years later, Finnish computer scientist Linus Torvalds created the free open-source operating system Linux, which now runs all the world's supercomputers. In 2012, the Egyptian scientist Dr. Nabil Ali was awarded Saudi Arabia's King Faisal Prize for his pioneering work in Arabic-language computing: he created programs that allowed computers to understand Arabic in digital form.

TWO

SEAS, SKIES, AND OUTER SPACE

THESE
KID INNOVATORS
USED THEIR
UNDERSTANDING OF THE ELEMENTS
* * **TO** * *
HARNESS POWER,
IMPROVE PEOPLE'S LIVES,
* * and * *
EXPLORE THE WORLD.

JACQUES COUSTEAU

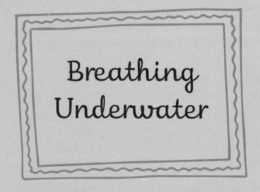

Breathing Underwater

Jacques Cousteau is known as the father of scuba diving. His invention allowed divers to breathe underwater, and his documentary films brought the undersea world into the homes of millions of people worldwide. But the first time he opened his eyes underwater, it was because of a childhood punishment.

Jacques Cousteau was born in 1910 in the village of St. André-de-Cubzac, near Bordeaux, France. His mother, Elizabeth, came from the town's wealthiest family; they had been wine merchants and landowners for generations. When Elizabeth was eighteen, she married Daniel, the son of the village's lawyer and a newly qualified lawyer himself. They had two sons: Pierre-Antoine and, four years later, Jacques-Yves.

Jacques's family enjoyed the luxuries of their wealth: yachts, parties, tennis, and travel. The family had an apartment in Paris but were rarely there. "My first conscious memory was of swaying in a hammock in a railway coach as the train steamed through the night," Jacques recalled.

When World War I broke out in 1914, life in Paris changed for the Cousteau family. Daniel's employer returned to the United States, and Daniel lost his job. Money was tight, and with the German army on the outskirts of the city, there was a shortage of food. Jacques developed stomach problems and grew very thin. Finally, the Cousteaus returned to St. André-de-Cubzac. Their home had no electricity, but at least here they would be able to grow vegetables on their land.

By the end of the war four years later, Jacques was a quiet child who felt uncomfortable with other kids and didn't like the games they played. In fact, he didn't seem to care about much at all. His parents worried, but they noticed that he seemed drawn to anything mechanical. He would happily spend hours in the garden, tinkering with bits of wood and using tree branches to move rocks around.

When Jacques was ten, his father was offered a job in New York City. The family set sail for an eight-day voyage across the Atlantic. Jacques loved it. He explored every inch of the ship and chatted to the stewards, engineers, and deck officers, who were delighted to show him around. His parents couldn't believe the change in his personality.

The Cousteau family moved into an apartment in New York. Daniel had to travel regularly for his work,

but Elizabeth decided to stay home to raise the boys. Pierre-Antoine started high school and Jacques went to Holy Name School. Pierre-Antoine was now going by the nickname PAC, and Jacques adopted the rhyming nickname of Jack—the American version of Jacques. Jack was shy, not fluent in English, and spoke with an accent. Fitting into a new school was hard. His brother was his best friend, and Jack relied on him heavily.

PAC was strong and athletic, but Jack struggled. He wasn't good at sports: he couldn't throw or catch well, he got out of breath running, and he hated boxing. He might still have been frail from his earlier health problems, but, more important, he just wasn't interested—and he couldn't be bothered with things that didn't interest him.

His early passion for mechanics had grown even stronger. He loved to build model boats and planes, which he displayed on shelves in his bedroom. When he was eleven years old, he came across a *Popular Mechanics* magazine that included plans for a scale model of a dock crane. He built it right away.

Once constructed, the crane was as tall as he was! It worked, too: using cranks and pulleys, it could swivel and lift objects. Jack improved on the original design, adding rotating pieces that allowed it to move backward and forward.

That summer, Jack's parents sent him to camp. Perhaps he needed more time with other kids, they thought, to help him get over his shyness. The campers spent their days canoeing, swimming, making crafts, and—to Jack's horror—riding horses. On the very first day, Jack fell off his horse. The instructor made him get back in the saddle, but as he sat there, with all the boys staring at him, Jack decided he would not be forced to do something he didn't want to do. He dismounted and refused to ride again. The instructor was furious with his open defiance—and the punishment he chose was something that changed the course of Jack's life.

The camp was near a muddy pond whose water was so dark that swimmers couldn't see the bottom. It was surrounded by trees that dropped leaves and branches into the water. The kids made up scary stories about the pond, and no one wanted the job of cleaning up the branches in the murky water. But that was exactly what Jack was ordered to do.

Jack stepped into the brown water and ducked below the surface—and for the first time ever, he opened his eyes underwater. It was too cloudy to see far, but Jack loved it. Beneath the surface, all was silent—the horses, his angry instructor, and the other boys suddenly seemed far away. Jack dove over and over, retrieving branches and swimming them to shore. He loved how the water felt against his skin, and he wondered if there was a way that he could breathe underwater—perhaps making a snorkel with the hollow reeds that grew near the pond.

By the time Jack was twelve, his father's employer decided to go back to France. Paris was recovering from the war. The family returned to their city apartment and the boys went back to school.

Before long, though, PAC left home for eighteen months of military service. Jack missed him terribly. At school, he was a loner. He still hated sports, he did badly in his classes, and he was socially awkward. He was happiest alone in his bedroom, where he could spend hours reading about technology and new inventions or building wooden models. Copying his brother, Jack adopted a new nickname based on his initials: JYC, pronounced Jeek.

At age fourteen, JYC discovered a new passion that would last a lifetime: filmmaking. After reading about this new art form, he saved his allowance for three months and bought a used hand-cranked movie camera called a Pathé Baby. These were among the first movie cameras made for home use. He wanted to understand how the camera worked, so before he shot his first roll of film, he spent hours taking it apart and reassembling it.

A month later, JYC filmed his cousin's wedding. At this time, moving pictures were new and very exciting. Everyone at the wedding was interested in the boy with the camera! But JYC was nervous. He had to develop his own film with jars of developer and fixer, and then splice the rolls of film together to make a continuous three-minute-long movie on one large reel. What if it didn't work? Everyone would think he was a failure!

But it worked perfectly. And having a camera made it easier to find friends: everyone wanted JYC to take their pictures. Soon, he was making films with plots, inventing heroes and villains, and experimenting with special effects.

School was still a problem, though. JYC disliked being stuck in a classroom, and his grades were terrible. His mother took away his camera as punishment. A week later, JYC was suspended after he was caught breaking windows. It had been an experiment, he said: he wanted to know if throwing a rock hard would make a bigger hole in the window than throwing a rock more gently.

JYC's parents decided to send him to a strict boarding school—without his camera. To their surprise, he loved it. He studied hard, got excellent marks, and graduated at the top of his class. But he wasn't sure what to do next. Filmmaking was a great hobby, but it was a hard way to earn a living. He had always wanted to fly, so he decided to join the navy and become an aviator.

Unfortunately, four years later, with his training just completed, JYC had a terrible car accident. Both of his arms were badly broken, and it seemed unlikely that he would ever fly again.

Then, an officer named Phillipe Talliez made a

suggestion: perhaps swimming would help his recovery. He took JYC to a rocky beach on France's Mediterranean coast. Phillipe spearfished while JYC exercised his arms in the water. One day, Phillipe persuaded JYC to try his mask and snorkel—and for the first time, he saw the undersea world. Algae-covered rocks, bright-green sea grass, schools of fish, sea urchins . . . He was in love with it all. "Sometimes we are lucky enough to know that our lives have been changed," he later reflected. "It happened to me on that summer's day, when my eyes were opened on the sea."

During World War II, Jacques Cousteau became a spy for the French Resistance. Between missions, he experimented with devices to allow him to breathe underwater—and he almost died twice! It was during this time that he met Emile Gagnan, a French engineer. With Jacques's practical experience and Gagnan's engineering skills, they teamed up and co-invented the Aqua-Lung. Finally, divers could swim freely and breathe without using diving bells or heavy helmeted suits. Their invention made scuba diving and underwater exploration possible.

Jacques Cousteau was also an innovator as a filmmaker. He gave millions of people their first glimpse of the underwater world: the brilliant colors of coral reefs and an endless variety of sea life. He also shared images that showed the dangers that plastic bags, nets, and abandoned fishing equipment posed to turtles, dolphins, and other creatures. "The reason I have made films about the undersea lies simply in my belief that people will protect what they love," he explained. "Yet we love only what we know."

WILBUR AND ORVILLE WRIGHT

The Brothers Who Wanted to Fly

Before the invention of the airplane, a trip across the United States took weeks, and a trip across the ocean even longer. Then, the Wright Brothers did what many thought impossible: they built a flying machine and achieved the first successful controlled flight. The world was forever changed.

Wilbur and Orville Wright were four years apart in age, but according to their father, they were as "inseparable as twins." Born in April 1867, Wilbur was the older of the pair. The boys had a younger sister, Katherine, and two brothers, Reuchlin and Lorin, who were nine and ten years older than Wilbur.

Their father, Milton, was bishop in the Church of the United Brethren in Christ, and he traveled frequently for work. Wilbur was born in Indiana and Orville in Ohio, and both boys were named after clergymen their father respected. The family moved a dozen times before finally settling in Dayton, Ohio, when the boys were teenagers.

The three youngest kids were known to most people as Will, Orv, and Katie, but they had special nicknames for one another. Wilbur was Ullam, Orville was Bubbo, and Katherine was Sterchens (from the German word *Schwerchens*, meaning "little sister"). People in the neighborhood often referred to them as just "the bishop's kids."

Their parents shared a love of learning. Susan, their mother, was intelligent and shy. The kids later described her as a "regular genius" who could make anything; Wilbur and Orville probably inherited their mechanical abilities from her. Susan's father had been a carriage maker, and she spent time in his workshop growing up. She made toys for her children, including a sled that they said was "as good as a store kind." She supported their interest in making things as well. Katherine later wrote, "She was the most understanding

woman. She recognized something unusual in Wilbur and Orville. . . . She never would destroy one thing the boys were trying to make. Any little thing they left around in her way she picked up and put on a shelf in the kitchen."

Their father was often away, but he also supported their curiosity, writing long letters home enthusiastically describing the places he was traveling through. Milton read widely and shared his ideas—along with advice on everything from money to behavior to character—with his children.

He also believed in the importance of toys and play as a way for kids to learn. When Wilbur and Orville were young, he brought home a souvenir from France: a little helicopter made from a stick of bamboo, with twin propellers powered by twisted rubber bands. It was based on a design by a French inventor named Alphonse Pénaud, whose work the boys would study as adults many years later. When released, the helicopter flew up to the ceiling. The brothers were excited and inspired by "the bat," as they called it. In first grade, Orville was already dreaming up ideas and building creations with wood while he sat at his desk. He told his teacher that he was constructing a machine that he and his brother could fly. By the time he was ten years old, he was making kites and selling them.

The Wrights valued learning and knew that not all education took place in a classroom. If Wilbur or Orville wanted to stay home to work on a project or read, their parents allowed them to. Everyone in the family read constantly, and their library was varied. There were shelves of novels and poetry; books about nature, history, travel; and two sets of encyclopedias. The children were encouraged to be open minded and think for themselves. Orville later said that their greatest advantage was "growing up in a family where there was always much encouragement to intellectual curiosity."

The brothers did well in school, but Orville had a mischievous streak and could be a troublemaker. In grades eight and nine, his teacher made him sit at the front of the class so that she could keep an eye on him.

He was cheerful and talkative but, like his mother, he could be shy with people he didn't know well. Wilbur was more serious; he had a remarkable memory and an ability to concentrate so deeply that he seemed off in his own world.

As a teenager, Wilbur had a serious injury. He was playing ice hockey when another boy hit him in the face with a hockey stick. The boy was known as a cruel bully, and his attack left Wilbur in excruciating pain. Wilbur had to get false teeth, and he became depressed. Before this incident, he had been in his last year of high school, earning outstanding marks in all subjects and excelling in football, skating, and gymnastics. He was planning to go to Yale University in Connecticut. But after his injuries, he dropped out of high school, staying home and reading the huge collection of books in their family library.

The brothers' mother's health was declining. She had been battling tuberculosis for years, and now she was very ill. Wilbur began caring for her, and as she grew weaker, he carried her upstairs to bed every night. On July 4, 1889, she died. She was fifty-eight years old.

Orville was still in high school, and earlier that year he had started his own print shop. In the carriage shed behind their house, he designed and built his first printing press, using a tombstone, a spring from a buggy, and scrap metal. Together, he and Wilbur began publishing a newspaper to share local news. When their mother died, they printed her obituary, writing that Susan Wright had been "very timid and averse to making any display in public, hence her true worth and highest qualities were most thoroughly appreciated by her family."

Wilbur, Orville, and Katherine were now aged 22, 17, and 14, and they still lived at home. They were devastated by the loss of their mother but pulled together to take care of one another. When Katherine moved out, becoming the only child in the family to go to college, Wilbur wrote to reassure her that they were managing on their own: "We have been living fine since you left. Orville cooks one week and I cook the next. Orville's week we have bread and butter and meat and gravy and coffee three times a day."

Around this time, bicycles were becoming popular, and cycling was the new trend. Some people were not happy about this new activity. Bicycles were distracting people from going to church or reading. Worst of all, many women rode bikes wearing "bloomers"—loose-fitting pants that were more practical than a dress but were, to some people, shockingly indecent.

Of course, most people were undeterred by these critics, especially Orville and Wilbur. They loved cycling and went for long rides together. In 1893, they opened their own business, selling and repairing bicycles. Cycling was all about balance and equilibrium, and the lessons the Wright brothers were learning would come in handy a few years later, when they began thinking about something that was widely considered impossible: human flight.

In 1896, Wilbur read about the death of Otto Lilienthal, a German man who had been building gliders and flying them with his younger brother. He was known as the "Flying Man," and his experiments captured Wilbur's imagination, reigniting the passion sparked by the childhood toy that he and Orville had called "the bat." Wilbur began reading about the theory of flight. Three years later, in a room above their bicycle shop, he and Orville built their first aircraft from bamboo and paper. Although it was a kite, it allowed them to test their design: a bi-plane with double wings, one above the other. The flight was successful enough that they decided to move on to the next step: a full-size glider that could carry the weight of a pilot.

In 1900, Orville and Wilbur traveled from Ohio to Kitty Hawk, North Carolina. The sand dunes by the ocean offered the steady wind their glider needed to take off and a soft surface to land on. First, they tested their designs with kites and no one aboard. Then they experimented with gliders, which they took turns piloting.

In 1903, the brothers added power to their invention, building an airplane called the *Wright Flyer I*. It had a gasoline engine and propellers that they designed and carved from wood. Orville and Wilbur tossed a coin to see who would fly first. Wilbur won—but his first attempt, on December 14, failed and damaged the plane. Three days later, after repairs, it was Orville's turn. He flew the plane—for twelve seconds about ten feet above the ground—and landed it successfully. Each brother flew twice that day—both wanted to pilot the world's first successful engine-powered airplane.

Wilbur and Orville Wright went on to design increasingly advanced planes that could fly faster, higher, and for longer distances—but their most important innovation may have been the control system they invented. It allowed the pilot to control the plane's movement in three dimensions—pitch, roll, and yaw—making it possible to steer and maintain balance. The Wrights' three-axis control system is still used in airplanes today, more than a hundred years later.

People have always been fascinated with the possibility of flight. Ancient Greek myths tell of Icarus, who made wings of wax and feathers but flew too close to the sun. Kids today build models based on the "ornithopter"—a flying machine designed by **Leonardo da Vinci** more than five hundred years ago. Leonardo may have been the first European to design a flying machine, but it was an Andalusian man of Berber descent who likely beat him by six hundred years. Abbas Ibn Firnas was a Muslim poet, inventor, engineer, chemist, and musician. Scholars believe that he designed and tested the first parachute, jumping from the tower of a mosque in the year 852. He broke a few bones but was undeterred: he later built and flew a glider made from wood and silk. Baghdad's Ibn Firnas airport is named after him, as is a crater on the moon.

WILLIAM KAMKWAMBA

Electric
Wind

William Kamkwamba survived a famine and was forced to drop out of his first year of high school. But he was curious and determined—and when he was only fourteen years old, he taught himself about electricity and built a windmill to bring power to his home in Malawi.

William was born in Dowa on August 5, 1987. His parents, Trywell and Agnes Kamkwamba, already had one daughter, and another arrived while William was still a baby. Agnes struggled to look after her three children, and at first Trywell did not help. He drank heavily and got into arguments. After being arrested for fighting in the local pub, he finally decided to change. He quit drinking and began supporting his family.

Trywell's older brother John had a farming business, and he invited Trywell to join him. So, William, his parents, and his sisters moved to a one-room house in Masitala village, Wimbe. John gave them a plot of land, so that they could grow tobacco to sell and vegetables to eat.

Their home was too small for the family, so after his long days in the fields, Trywell worked to build a bigger two-room house. The family lived in the new house for three years. Now, William had five sisters: Annie, Dorris, Rose, Aisha, and Mayless. Fortunately, by this time Trywell could afford to hire workers to help construct two new buildings. At last, William had a room of his own. He described it as his "hideaway" where he could think and daydream.

As a child, William knew little about technology. "Before I discovered the miracles of science, magic ruled the word," he later wrote. He began his autobiography with the story of his earliest memory. He was six years old, playing in the road, when some older boys came along. They had a giant bag full of gum balls—and William loved gum. The boys gave him a handful and William quickly stuffed them into his mouth.

But the next day, something terrifying happened. William overheard a trader talking to his father and learned that the trader had dropped the bag of gum balls, which the boys had taken. "I've gone to see the *sing'anga*," the trader said, "and whoever ate that gum will soon be sorry." The sing'anga was the witch doctor—and William was sure he was going to die. He ran to his father and confessed that he had eaten the gum. "I don't want to die, Papa," he sobbed.

His father told him not to worry. Then he walked five miles to the trader's home, explained what had happened, and paid for the bag of gum. "We were just in time," he told his son, laughing.

Growing up, William was close to his cousin Geoffrey and his friend Gilbert. "We were a solid gang of three," he recalled. "We all loved trucks, and each week, we'd compete to see who could build the biggest and strongest one." They collected empty drink cartons to use as the bodies of the trucks and added bottle caps for the wheels.

Eventually, they decided to make more ambitious, go-cart-style vehicles called chigirigiri. Once they'd built them, they held "monster derbies," racing one another down the road.

When William was nine years old, his uncle John died, and William's family had to survive on their own.

At this time, the lives of farmers in Malawi were becoming more difficult. Big companies were producing tobacco, and it was hard for small farms to compete. His family had little money and meat was expensive, so William began hunting for birds with his cousins.

William's dog Khamba loved going hunting with him. He was white, with black spots that made him look like someone had splattered him with paint. It was unusual to have a dog as a pet in Malawi, but William enjoyed Khamba's company. "It was nice having someone around, especially someone who didn't talk or tell me what to do," he said.

William's village had no electricity, so battery-operated radios were the only connection to the larger world. "From the first time I heard the sounds coming

from the radio, I wanted to know what was going on inside," he recalled. When William was thirteen, he and Geoffrey started taking apart radios to figure out how they worked. They learned through trial and error—"a great many radios were sacrificed for our knowledge," he admitted. After a while, people began bringing their broken radios for the boys to fix, and soon they had a small business. People called them "little scientists." If scientists solved the mysteries of how things worked, William decided, then a scientist was what he wanted to be.

But in December 2000, everything started to go wrong—not just for William, but for the entire country of Malawi. Heavy rain caused flooding that destroyed crops, and this was followed by a drought. William's family lost half of their corn crop. They worried about how they would survive the next year.

One thing that distracted William from the looming disaster was his discovery of the bicycle dynamo—a gadget that allows the rider's pedaling to power a bike light. He wondered how it worked. Could it be used to power a radio? Sure enough, it could! As William pedaled, the radio played music, and Geoffrey started dancing. William then had another question: What could do the pedaling *for* him so that he and Geoffrey could dance at the same time?

Soon, however, no one felt like dancing at all. A terrible famine was overtaking the country. Floods and drought were partly to blame for the crops wilting in the fields, but the Malawi government made the food crisis worse by selling all the surplus grain. Traders who did have grain raised their prices. People lined up for hours in hopes of buying food. William's family cut back to two meals a day, and then to just one.

Adding to his family's stress was the birth of another baby girl. Fortunately, she was healthy, and they named her Tiyamike, meaning "Thank God." But there was little else to be thankful for. Everyone in the family was growing thin, and all around them people were starving.

Despite growing up during this difficult time, William was excited to start secondary school that January. Unfortunately, his low grades meant that he had to go to the worst school in the district. The school had no desks, so students sat on the floor. He vowed to study hard so that he could transfer to a better school, but it was difficult to focus with his stomach twisting with hunger. Some students stopped going to class; they were too weak to walk to school. By February, William's family had no money to pay the school fees, and he was forced to drop out.

After months of suffering, the family finally saw a sign of hope. By March, their corn crop was growing, with tall stalks and ripening cobs. Every day, William and Geoffrey checked to see if they were ready to eat— and at last, it was time to harvest. "That afternoon, Geoffrey and I probably ate thirty ears," William said.

The family had come frighteningly close to disaster, but now they knew they would survive. William still couldn't go to school, but he wanted to learn. He began visiting the small library at the primary school. He read books about hydroelectricity and how turbines could be used to generate power. He learned about magnetism, electric motors, and AC and DC currents. Some of the words were new, but the ideas made perfect sense: the spinning motion created power, just like the bicycle dynamo!

In one book, William saw a picture of a windmill. He remembered wondering what could pedal a bike to power a radio so that he and Geoffrey could dance, and here was the answer: the wind. William began visiting the scrapyard and collected bicycle parts, steering wheels, and gearboxes from old cars and tractors, which he could modify to meet his needs. It was a huge project, and there were many challenges to overcome, but Gilbert and Geoffrey helped and eventually everything was ready. The boys used ropes and a pulley—made from William's mother's clothesline—to raise the machine onto a sixteen-foot-high wooden tower. Curious people gathered around, asking what this contraption was. There was no word for windmill in his language, so William replied, "Electric wind." He held a light bulb in his hand and waited for the wind to turn the blades. Would it work?

It did! The crowd cheered. But William wasn't finished. He used the windmill to light up his bedroom, and then to power the lights and radio in his family's home. The story caught the attention of the media and began to spread around the world. William was invited to do a TED talk, and he spoke about his dream of

building a larger windmill: one that could provide irrigation for the whole village. Many people were inspired by his words and wanted to support his work.

Over the next few years, William built a solar-powered water pump to provide clean water in his village, two more wind turbines, and a drip irrigation system. He returned to school, completed a university degree, and wrote a book about his life, which was made into a movie called *The Boy Who Harnessed the Wind*. His story has inspired millions of people around the world.

ELON MUSK

Electric Cars and Rockets to Mars

Elon Musk's innovations include electric cars, solar roofs, and SpaceX rockets. An erratic and controversial figure, Elon has nonetheless captured the public's imagination with his talk of colonizing Mars and wild publicity stunts, like launching a Tesla into space. But before pursuing his passions, he had to overcome bullying and start a new life thousands of miles from home.

Elon was born in 1971 and grew up in the South African city of Pretoria. During the 1970s, South Africa was governed under a system of white supremacy and racial segregation known as apartheid. As a white boy from a relatively wealthy family, Elon had far more privilege than most people in his country. But he grew up in a climate of constant tension and frequent violence in a country that he knew was viewed negatively by much of the world.

When Elon was born, his family had lived in South Africa for twenty years. His great-grandmother may have been the first chiropractor in Canada. Elon was her husband's middle name, and her son Joshua was Elon's grandfather. Joshua was an eccentric man who taught himself to fly, bought a plane, and took his family on trips all over North America. In 1950, they moved to South Africa, where their adventures continued: Joshua and his wife, Wyn, are thought to be the only private pilots to fly from South Africa to Australia in a single-engine plane. They took Elon's father, Errol, on long trips into the African bush, searching for the mythological Lost City of the Kalahari Desert. Joshua died when Elon was a toddler, but Elon grew up hearing about his travels. "My grandmother told these tales of how they almost died several times along their journeys," he recalled.

Elon's mother, Maye, met Errol when they were kids.

Maye liked math and science, became a model, and was a finalist in the Miss South Africa pageant. She and Errol dated while in college and then married. Errol was an engineer, and Maye worked as a dietician. Elon was born nine months after their wedding, and his brother Kimbal and sister Tosca came along soon after.

Elon was a curious and energetic toddler. "He seemed to understand things quicker than the other kids," his mother said. Still, she worried. Sometimes Elon would stare off into space, not responding when people spoke to him. She thought that perhaps he was deaf. The doctors ran tests and even removed his adenoid glands, which was thought to improve children's hearing. But Elon continued to go off into these trance-like states. According to his mother, he still does. "Now, I just leave him be because I know he's designing a new rocket or something," she said.

Elon explained that, as a child, he realized he could block out everything and concentrate on whatever he was thinking about. His mind works visually: he can see images in great detail. "It seems as though the part of my brain that's usually reserved for visual processing . . . gets taken over by internal thought processes," he has said. "I can't do this as much now because there are so many things demanding my attention, but as a kid it happened a lot."

Unfortunately, Elon's quirkiness didn't make him popular. Other kids disliked being ignored and thought he was rude or too different. Once, when a young relative complained of being scared of the dark, Elon simply responded that "dark was merely the absence of light"—which might be true, but wasn't very helpful! Elon had a tendency to correct people, which wasn't always appreciated. Being highly logical, he thought people would want to know about flaws in their thinking, but kids just didn't want to play with him anymore. Even his brother and sister preferred not to include him. "Mom, he's not fun," they would say.

Elon was also strong-willed. When he was about six years old, he wanted to go to his cousin's party but his mother had grounded him. Elon decided he would walk. "I sort of thought I knew the way, but it was clear across town," he recalled. In fact, it was much farther than he realized—more than ten miles away. The journey took him about four hours. Just as his mom was leaving the party with his brother and sister, she spotted Elon walking down the road! Knowing that he was supposed to be at home, Elon panicked. "I then sprinted to my cousin's house . . . and climbed a tree and refused to come down," he said.

As a kid, Elon always had a book in his hands. His brother said he would often read for ten hours a day. Sometimes, when the family was out shopping, Elon would disappear—they would find him in the nearest bookstore, sitting on the floor reading. After school, he used to go to the bookstore and stay there for hours. "Sometimes they kicked me out of the store, but usually not," he recalled. He read everything but especially loved science fiction. *The Lord of the Rings* and *The*

Hitchhiker's Guide to the Galaxy were among his favorites.

When he was in third or fourth grade, Elon started to read the *Encyclopedia Britannica*. "That was so helpful," he said. "You don't know what you don't know. You realize that there are all these things out there." And Elon had an incredible memory for all those things! If anyone in the family had a question, his sister Tosca would say, "Just ask genius boy." But this didn't make him any more popular with the kids at school. They thought he was a know-it-all.

Elon's parents divorced when he was about eight years old. Maye and the children moved to Durban, on South Africa's east coast. Two years later, Elon decided to move in with his father: "My father seemed sort of sad and lonely," he said. "My mom had three kids [with her] and he didn't have any. It seemed unfair." His brother Kimbal later followed.

In some ways, life at their father's house was comfortable. They had plenty of money, they traveled a lot, Elon had books, and he learned engineering skills at his dad's work sites: wiring, bricklaying, and more. But his father was not easy to live with. Many years later, Elon described him as a "terrible human being." He used to sit Elon and his brother down and lecture them for hours. Elon said that while there were some good times, "it was not a happy childhood. It was like misery."

The first time Elon saw a computer was in an electronics store when he was ten years old. It was around 1981, and computers weren't yet commonplace. Elon immediately began begging his father to buy one and was thrilled when Errol brought home a Commodore VIC-20. It came with a programming workbook, and Elon worked for three days straight, barely pausing to sleep. He said it was the "most super-compelling thing" he had ever seen.

Some of Elon's engineering and entrepreneurial interests emerged when he was young. He started making rockets, buying various chemicals and combining them inside metal canisters: "It is remarkable how many things you can get to explode,"

Elon later said. "I'm lucky I have all my fingers." He also launched businesses with his brother and cousins. They sold Easter eggs door to door and tried to start their own video arcade. That plan fell apart when they realized none of them were old enough to sign the necessary legal documents.

Elon loved science fiction and fantasy, and he wrote stories about dragons and other creatures. He was also passionate about computer games—both playing them and making them. When he was twelve, a South African magazine called *PC and Office Technology* published the code for a space-battle video game he created called Blastar, earning Elon $500.

But his school life was difficult. Elon was being bullied and beaten up by other boys. Once, he was hurt so badly that he had to go the hospital and missed a week of classes. Luckily, he had close relationships with his brother Kimbal and his cousins. When he was not at school, they spent hours playing Dungeons and Dragons, with Elon taking the lead as an imaginative and inspiring Dungeon Master.

The situation improved in grade ten, when Elon transferred to Pretoria Boys High School. He was a quiet student who didn't do particularly well academically. He later explained that he didn't see the point in learning things he wasn't interested in. In fact,

when he was in fourth and fifth grade, he used to get
failing grades until his mother's boyfriend warned that
he could be held back. "I didn't know you had to pass
subjects to move to the next grade," he said. Even in
high school, he worked hard only on the subjects that
mattered to him, like physics and computers. "There
needs to be a reason for a grade. I'd rather play video
games, write software, and read books than try and get
an A if there's no point in getting an A," he said. More
important than grades, Elon thought, was trying to
understand the meaning and purpose of life. "In the
comics, it always seems like they are trying to save the
world," he said. "It seemed like one should try to make
the world a better place."

When Elon was seventeen, he applied for Canadian

citizenship. As soon as he got his passport, he flew to Canada. He didn't have much of a plan, but he thought he would have more opportunities in North America. He spent a year working odd jobs around the country:

tending vegetables, chopping logs with a chainsaw, and cleaning out the steaming-hot boiler room at a lumber mill. Meanwhile, his mother, brother, and sister were trying to join him. Maye flew to Canada to look for a place to live, while fourteen-year-old Tosca sold Elon's car and put their house up for sale. By 1989, the family was reunited, and Elon had enrolled in a university.

During the next few years, Elon found people who shared his interests in science and business, and he began to think about what he wanted to do in life. He loved making video games, but he wanted to have a bigger effect on the world—to do something that would improve humanity's future. Three areas stood out: renewable energy, the internet, and space. Elon pursued them all, founding such companies as Tesla, PayPal, and SpaceX. He says he would eventually like to die on Mars . . . just not on impact!

THREE

CRACKING CODES AND SAVING LIVES

* * * **FROM** * * *

CHANGING THE
COURSE OF WAR

* **TO** *

PIONEERING
MEDICAL ADVANCES

THAT HAVE

SAVED MILLIONS OF LIVES,

THESE

KID INNOVATORS

SHOW THAT

SMALL THINGS
CAN MAKE A
BIG DIFFERENCE.

ALAN TURING

Code-Breaking Hero of World War II

Alan Turing is best known for breaking the Enigma Code that was used by Nazi Germany to send secret messages during the Second World War. He also designed the first digital computer and is considered one of the fathers of computer science and artificial intelligence.

Alan was born in London, England, but his parents met on a ship crossing the Pacific from India to the United States. Julius Turing and Ethel Sara Stoney fell in love before the ship reached Japan, and after visiting Yellowstone National Park together, they got married in Ireland. At this time, India was under British rule, and many English people lived and worked there. Julius and Ethel returned to India after their wedding, and their first child, John, was born there. Alan came along four years later, in 1912, shortly after the family returned to England for a period of leave. When Alan was one year old, his parents went back to live in India. They were worried that the hot climate there would be bad for the children's health, so Alan and his brother were sent to live with a retired couple in the British coastal town of St Leonards-on-Sea.

Colonel Ward and Mrs. Ward lived in a large house called Baston Lodge with their four daughters, including Hazel, whom Alan liked very much, and Joan, whom he despised. Colonel Ward was kind but distant, and Mrs. Ward, whom they called Grannie, expected the boys to act in stereotypically male ways: to be "real men." She was disappointed that they were not interested in playing with guns, model battleships, and other toy weapons. She even wrote to their mother complaining that John was a bookworm.

Alan and his brother passed their days walking along the windy waterfront or having picnics on the beach. Their evenings were spent sitting in front of cozy fires in the nursery, where they were looked after by Nanny Thompson. When Alan was three and John was six, their mother returned from India for the summer. She later recalled Alan's earliest experiment from that time: a toy sailor was broken, so Alan planted the arms and legs in the garden, hoping they would grow into new toy sailors.

Alan's experiments were often not appreciated by the adults in the house. He was considered to be a cheeky child and was often in trouble with his mother, Nanny Thompson, and Mrs. Ward. He spoke very well for his age and made up some creative phrases—for example, instead of saying "for a long time" he would say "for so many morrows." Like many small children, though, Alan had tantrums when he didn't get his own way. When his mother returned to India in the fall, she said to Alan, "You'll be a good boy, won't you?" Alan replied honestly: "Yes, but sometimes I shall forget!"

The next spring, Alan's parents visited. This time, his mother decided to stay in England for three years. John was sent away to boarding school, and Alan, now four, lived with his mother in St Leonards. She loved to paint and she took Alan to her sketching parties, where the little boy—with his big eyes and sailor hat—would often be the center of attention among the young art students. Alan's mother also took him to the Anglican church every weekend for the communion service. This was much less enjoyable. There was always incense burning, and Alan didn't like it at all: he called it "the church with the bad smells."

Yuck!

Alan taught himself to read in just three weeks, and when it came to learning numbers, he was even quicker. The lampposts in St Leonards were marked with serial numbers, and Alan insisted on stopping at each one to read the numbers aloud. What he found much harder to grasp was the concept of left and right. So, he came up with a creative solution: he made a small red mark on his left thumb and called it his "knowing spot."

When Alan was six, he started school. He was expected to learn Latin, which did not interest him at all, and like many kids, he found handwriting very difficult. It didn't help that children at this time had to learn to write with scratchy, leaky fountain pens. Alan's notebooks were always full of crossed-out words and ink splotches. He loved maps, though. He asked for an atlas for his birthday and spent many hours studying it.

Alan also loved nature books. He invented a mixture to cure nettle stings and carefully recorded the list of ingredients. And he liked making up words: He called the cries of the seagulls quockling instead of squawking and coined the word greasicle for the melted wax around the wick of a candle.

When Alan was seven, his mother returned to India to be with her husband, and Alan stayed behind with Colonel Ward and Grannie. He wrote to his parents, describing new concoctions he was inventing—like "gobletoe drink," a mixture of grass, radish leaves, and nettles, which he said was "very sweet." At age eight, he decided to write a book called *About a Microscope*. His mother described it as "the shortest scientific work on record"—it consisted of only one sentence: "First you must see that the lite is rite."

At this time, Alan's brother John was away at boarding school, and nine-year-old Alan was sent to join him there. Their mother was concerned that Alan was becoming too "unsociable and dreamy." Alan spent most of his spare time making paper boats. He disliked sports and later said that he learned to be a fast runner because he was desperate to get away from the ball. He was teased about his daydreaming, studying the daisies during field hockey games and calculating geometric angles on the football field. He did enjoy acting in a school play, and he liked chess very much.

Alan also liked inventing things. In a letter to his parents, he wrote: "Guess what I am writing with. It is an invention of my own it is a fountain pen like this"— and he provided a diagram to illustrate how his new pen worked. In another letter, he described his idea for a typewriter. If he had been able to use one, his life would have been easier: handwriting continued to be a problem, despite his hard work to improve it. At age twelve, he discovered an encyclopedia at school, and after being given some chemicals and equipment for Christmas, he began using it to teach himself organic chemistry.

When Alan was fourteen, he enrolled at Sherborne School. The start of the term coincided with a general strike in England. Many buses and trains were not running, so Alan decided he would bicycle the sixty miles to school. His adventurous arrival impressed the staff and students and was unusual enough to be reported in the local paper.

But things did not go so well after that: Alan found it hard to fit in at his new school. He was bullied by other boys and by some teachers as well. His appearance was messy, with his hair always flopping over his face, his shirts untucked, and his hands stained with ink.

Alan did not do well in his classes, either. He had a habit of ignoring subjects that didn't interest him. Even in math, he would experiment with advanced ideas while neglecting the more basic work that teachers expected him to complete. One teacher, who caught him doing algebra when he was supposed to be studying religion, wrote in his report that Alan's writing was the worst he had ever seen, his work was "slipshod and dirty," and he was "ludicrously behind." Another teacher said that he'd donate a billion pounds to charity if Alan passed Latin. (Alan passed, but the teacher did not follow through on his vow.)

Alan went on to become a brilliant mathematician, cryptanalyst, computer scientist, philosopher, and theoretical biologist. He had a talent for making connections between seemingly unrelated areas. In the late 1930s, he invented the Turing machine—a theoretical model of a computer. During the World War II, he worked at Bletchley Park, Britain's top-secret code-breaking center. He designed a decryption device and played a lead role in cracking the Enigma code—a secret code used by Nazi Germany. His work helped Britain win the war. Without him, the war might have gone on for much longer, and many more people could have been killed. After the war ended, Alan worked on the design of a new computer: The ACE, or Automatic Computing Engine, was the first detailed design for a computer that could store programs electronically. He also wrote about intelligent machinery, and developed what he called the "imitation game." This was a test in which a person would have a typed conversation with a computer, and an observer would try to distinguish the human from the machine. If they could not, then the computer had passed what later became known as the Turing Test.

Despite his incredible contributions to his country, the British government turned on him. Alan Turing was a gay man living at a time when this was against the law in the United Kingdom. In 1952, he was arrested because of his relationship with another man. He had never much cared about the opionions of others, and he did not deny being gay: He thought the law was absurd and should be changed. But he was treated as a criminal. He also lost his security clearance and was no longer trusted to do important, secret work. Two years later, he died by suicide at age forty-one.

In recent years, the British government has officially apologized for the terrible way he was treated, and Queen Elizabeth II issued a pardon. His legacy is now celebrated, and in 2021, the Bank of England issued a new British fifty-pound note, featuring the face of Alan Turing.

More than 10,000 people worked at Bletchley Park, and most of them were women. They did many jobs, including running the Bombe decryption devices invented by Alan Turing. Decrypting enemy messages was work usually done by men, but most men were away fighting. So recruiters looked for women who might make good codebreakers. They even approached the winners of a crossword competition held by the newspaper!

One woman who played an important role was **Mavis Lilian Batey**. She was only nineteen years old when she was recruited to work as a codebreaker. Her previous job had been looking for coded spy messages in the personal columns of the newspaper. At Bletchley Park, she deciphered a message from the Italian navy that revealed an enemy plan to attack a convoy of British navy supply ships. She also deciphered German messages, which allowed her team to break two Enigma machines—encryption devices that many had thought were unbreakable.

HEDY LAMARR

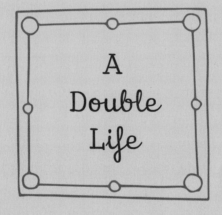

A
Double
Life

F or decades, most of the world knew Hedy
Lamarr only as a Hollywood star, but she
was also a self-taught inventor. The technology
she developed helped lead to the wireless
networks used by cell phones today.

Hedy was born Hedwig Eva Maria Keisler in Vienna, Austria, on November 9, 1914. World War I had begun just months before, but Hedy's childhood was barely touched by the larger events unfolding around her. Her father, Emil Kiesler, was from a Jewish family in West Ukraine. Her mother, Gertrud—or Trude, as she was called—was born in Hungary. Like Emil, Trude was born into a Jewish family, but she had converted to Catholicism.

Emil managed a bank, and the couple was wealthy. Soon after their baby's birth, they moved to a luxurious apartment in a residential part of the city. Hedwig's dad nicknamed her Hedylendelein and her mom called her Hedl. When the little girl learned to talk, she couldn't quite say her full name, and so she became Hedy.

As a child, Hedy loved pretty things: lace, velvet, sweet-smelling flowers. She liked watching her mother get ready to go out. "When I was tiny," Hedy later recalled, "I loved to watch her dress her hair, use her scents and powders, try on this gown and that until she found the one which suited her mood for the evening." In fact, Hedy's parents went out most evenings, going to the opera or the theater and enjoying the exciting nightlife of Vienna. Hedy was safe at home and always well-looked after, but she later recalled having horrible nightmares on those nights.

The family had a nurse, a cook, and a maid, and these adults played an important role in caring for Hedy. Although they were busy, Hedy's parents adored her. Her father called her Princess Hedy, and he made sure she always had everything she needed. He took her on long walks in the Vienna woods, played make-believe games with her, and told her stories. "He'd unfold his hand, as if it were a book, look at his palm and begin his story," she remembered. "I was enchanted." If Emil was home in the evening, he would read to her in front of the fireplace or when he tucked her in to bed. He noticed that she was inquisitive and curious about how things worked, so as they walked around town, he explained the technology behind the things they saw, "from printing presses to street cars."

Hedy led a privileged life. She took ballet and piano lessons, and she was taught German, Italian, and French by her governess Nicolette, whom Hedy called Nixy. Her mother worried that Hedy would be spoiled, and she tried not to praise her too much. Everything Hedy did, according to Trude, was just "all right." Trude wanted Hedy to enjoy simple things as well as luxuries, and so she was allowed to have a dog and was given chores to do, like caring for the family's birds and keeping the birdcage clean.

When Hedy was five, she learned to read. She soon discovered movie magazines. "I had a little stage under my father's desk where I would act out fairy tales," she recalled. "I was always talking to myself." Hedy used to dress up in her mother's clothes, or her dad's suits and hats, and act out scenes from movies. Because she was an only child, she often played alone or with her dolls. Her favorite doll was a blond one that she called Beccacine. Her uncle once teased her by saying that Beccacine was "only a doll." Hedy was furious. "I hated him after that," she said. Beccacine traveled all over the world with Hedy, even when she was an adult.

As she got older, Hedy's parents often took her on their travels: to the opera in Rome, to the streets and shops of Paris, to explore the English countryside, or to go walking in the Swiss Alps. During school vacations, the family went to their summer home in Salzburg. They traveled to the countryside on the weekends to play tennis or swim. In the winters, they went to

Switzerland for skiing and ice skating. Hedy later remembered these as the happiest times in her life.

During the 1920s, anti-Semitism, or prejudice against Jewish people, was rising, and Hedy's parents were worried. Hedy was raised Catholic, and she kept her Jewish heritage secret throughout her life. When she was nearly fifteen, she was sent to a girls' finishing school in Lucerne, Switzerland. The school was supposed to teach the girls discipline and etiquette; they were expected to marry, not work. It was very strict, and Hedy was miserable. She ran away repeatedly. One time, she fled the school because she didn't want to eat rhubarb! "I didn't like the stuff and refused to eat it," she said. "They told me I would get nothing else to eat unless I did. So I ran away." But she was always found and brought back.

Finally, Hedy came up with a plan. She asked a friend in Vienna to send a message to the school, pretending to be her parents and claiming that she was needed at home. The headmistress was fooled, and Hedy was able to book her passage to Vienna by train. Once back in the family home, Hedy managed to persuade her parents not to make her return to Switzerland. She spent her allowance on movie magazines and went to the cinema as often as she could. Without her parents' knowledge, she entered a beauty contest and won. "She knew what she wanted," Trude said. "What she wanted was not, always, what we wanted for her. . . . But she did not ask for advice, or, I must admit, permission. She did not need to, I suppose, because she always knew where she was going."

Hedy's parents hoped they could steer her away from acting. They enrolled her in a school in Vienna where she could study art and design. On her way there, she walked past the Sascha Film Studio—Vienna's first film studio, built in 1916. Hedy asked her mother if she could write a note excusing her from school for one hour to run an errand. Her mom agreed. Then Hedy secretly took a pen and added a zero, changing one hour to ten hours, and gave the note to her teacher. The teacher pointed out that the note was for two full days. "Yes," Hedy said, "I know."

After school that day, Hedy went to the film studio and said she wanted a job. She had two days to prove herself. By the end of the first day, she had a small non-speaking part, sitting in a nightclub wearing a black evening gown. So, she went home and told her parents that she was going to quit school and work at the film studio. Breaking into acting was not easy, and Hedy's path was a difficult one, but she was determined. By the time she was twenty-four, she was living in Hollywood and being hailed by the press as the world's most beautiful woman.

Hedy Lamarr went on to make many films, but few people knew what she did when she wasn't acting. She invented things. Hedy set up an inventor's corner in her Hollywood home, with a drafting table to work at. She designed an improved traffic stoplight, and she made a tablet that could be dissolved in water to make a carbonated drink (she said it tasted terrible). "Inventions are easy for me to do," she explained. "I don't have to work on ideas, they come naturally."

When World War II broke out in 1941, Hedy wanted to help. She learned that the radio-controlled torpedoes used by the U.S. Navy could be jammed and sent off course by the enemy, so she came up with an idea for a "frequency hopping signal" that couldn't be jammed. Working with her friend George Antheil, she developed and patented a device and offered it to the Navy. The Navy, however, was not interested in inventions by outsiders—and certainly not ones designed by Hollywood actresses. Twenty years later, however, they installed an updated version of her design on Navy ships.

It wasn't until she was over eighty years old that the world learned that Hedy Lamarr was an innovator as well as an actress. In 1997, she was given the Electronic Frontier Foundation Pioneer Award as well as the BULBIE Gnass Spirit of Achievement Bronze Award. The BULBIE is considered the Oscar of the inventing world, and she was the first woman to win it. The technology she worked on helped make possible the secure wireless networks, GPS, and Bluetooth now used around the world. Although she was famous for her beauty—her face was said to have inspired Disney's Snow White—it is her contributions to communications technology that are her lasting legacy. As she said, "The brains of people are more interesting than the looks I think."

JONAS SALK

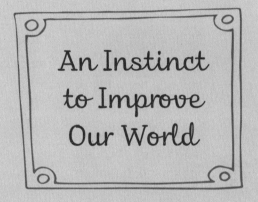

An Instinct
to Improve
Our World

F or the first half of the twentieth century,
people lived in fear of polio. Many died from
the disease, and even more were left paralyzed
by it. Most of those affected were children.
Today, polio has been nearly wiped out, thanks
to a worldwide vaccination campaign—and to
Jonas Salk, who created the first polio vaccine.

Jonas was born on October 28, 1914, and raised in the Bronx. From the moment of his birth, his mother, Dora, was convinced that he was special. He was born with a caul—a piece of membrane covering his head. That happens rarely—only one in every 80,000 births—and it is seen by some as a sign of good luck. Dora believed it was an indication that her child was destined for greatness.

You're so special!

Dora and her husband, Daniel, were Jewish, and both of their families had come to the United States to escape persecution. Dora was from Russia, where there had been an organized campaign of violence against Jewish people. In 1903, when she was thirteen years old, Dora and her family arrived in New York. Like many new immigrants, they were very poor. Dora was intelligent but had no access to school in America. As a young teen, she started work in a garment factory and quickly moved up into management.

Daniel was born in the United States, but his parents had come from Lithuania. Like Dora's family, they had endured the anti-Semitism of the Russian czars. Daniel was a successful lace maker and designer of women's clothing. He and Dora married in 1912, and Jonas was born two years later. Their home was near a park and just a few blocks away from Bronx Park, which had botanical gardens and a zoo.

Jonas was almost two years old when the 1916 polio epidemic hit the city and then spread to neighboring states. It was terrifying: no one knew what caused the illness or where it would strike next. Parents kept their children home. By August, hospitals were overflowing and every isolation bed in the city was in use. Twenty-seven thousand people died that summer—and in New York City, 80 percent of the dead were children under five. Many who survived were left paralyzed. For some, that meant a weakened leg; for others, it meant relying on machines known as "iron lungs" to help them breathe.

Jonas escaped unharmed, but for the next forty years, summer was known as polio season. Pools and play-grounds closed, and millions of frightened parents held their breath and hoped their children would be spared.

Jonas was a quiet and gentle child, more like his easygoing father than his more intense mother. He loved to read; one of his relatives later recalled that "Jonas was always in a book." Luckily, the New York Public Library had just started a traveling library program that brought books right into his neighborhood. Dora made sure he always had plenty to read.

When Jonas was five, his brother Herman was born. The two boys were very different: Herman was as talkative as Jonas was quiet, and while Jonas usually did as he was told without complaint, Herman was more rebellious. Jonas didn't always appreciate his brother interrupting him and wanting to play.

Luckily, Jonas was now old enough to start school. He was small for his age, curly-haired and thin, and he already wore glasses. He was also highly intelligent. In fact, his teachers were so impressed with his ability and interest in learning that Jonas ended up skipping several grades. He was a serious child and didn't often play with other kids: "I tended to observe and reflect and wonder," he later said. "I kept pretty much to myself."

At dinner, there were arguments. Dora would pile food on the boys' plates and insist that they eat it all. Herman would refuse, but Jonas was more indirect in how he resisted: he would put the food in his mouth, leave the table, and spit it out! Although he avoided conflict, he did dream of being freer. He remembered thinking that someday he would grow up and do something in his own way, without anyone telling him how.

When Jonas was about twelve, a third brother, Lee, was born. But Jonas was always Dora's favorite, and he knew it. "I was the eldest of three sons, and the favorite, and the one who had all of her attention," he later said. He and his mother spent hours talking about current events and the news, about money, and about his future. Sometimes, Dora could be controlling, and her expectations could feel suffocating, but Jonas never doubted that he was loved.

Later in life, Jonas reflected that Dora had wanted the best for him. "My mother had no schooling. She came to this country from Russia in 1901 [and] . . . as a young girl, began to work and would help to support the family. She was very ambitious, in a sense, for her children. She wanted her children to have more than she had, so that she lived her life and invested her life to live through her children."

During his childhood, Jonas had several experiences

that made a deep impression on him. When he was about four, he saw an Armistice Day parade and was puzzled to see the soldiers who were missing an arm or a leg. When he started school, he saw many children who had survived polio, wearing leg braces. And as a Jewish child, he was aware of anti-Semitism—both from the stories of his relatives and all around him in the United States. These experiences made him interested in larger questions about life. "I think that we have an instinct, an impulse to improve our world. And I think that's quite universal," he later said.

Jonas's religious beliefs were also a source of his desire to do good in the world. Every day, he prayed that he would be able to contribute something important, that he would make a difference. "I became aware of a desire to do something in life that would help relieve some of the suffering," he said. His brothers teased him, but Jonas was undeterred. "The remainder of childhood was for me a period of patient waiting," he said.

Jonas started high school at age twelve, attending a competitive all-boys school called Townsend Harris Hall. The school was on the campus of New York's City College, the first free college in the country. For the first time, he was surrounded by students as smart as—or even smarter than—he was. Most were from immigrant families, and the majority were Jewish. The school didn't teach chemistry or biology, but Jonas was fine with that. "I was not interested in science," he said. What he loved best was literature. He read Emerson, Thoreau, Lincoln, and Francis Bacon. He was a deep thinker, drawn to ideas and philosophy.

In October 1929, the U.S. stock market crashed, sending the country into the decade-long Great Depression. People lost their savings, their jobs, and even their houses. Many relied on soup kitchens and breadlines to survive. Jonas had just turned fifteen, and the suffering he saw affected him greatly. He decided that he would become a lawyer so he could fight injustice and work for change. He joined his school's Current History Society and its Law and Debate Society; he also arranged talks by local officials and visited the city courts. But he didn't tell his friends about his goals, choosing to keep his plans private.

A year later, just before his sixteenth birthday, Jonas started college. He was the first in his family to do so.

Like most of his classmates, he went to City College because it was free. It was also highly competitive, with many students wanting to do law and medicine. After getting mediocre grades in his first semester, Jonas started working harder. He didn't join clubs or take part in sports, and although friendly, he was self-contained and private. "He was awfully difficult to know well," one of his classmates said.

Finally, Jonas told his mother about his dream of studying law. She thought it was a terrible idea. "[My] mother didn't think I'd make a very good lawyer. Her reasons were that I couldn't really win an argument with her," Jonas said. So he switched from pre-law to pre-medical courses, and discovered that, although he had not been interested in science before, he found chemistry fascinating. His mother thought he should be a teacher, instead; he wasn't strong enough for medicine, she said. But this time, Jonas didn't listen. He applied to medical school against her wishes.

Jonas already knew he didn't want a traditional career as a doctor: he was more interested in the science of medicine than the practice of it. At one of his medical school interviews, a professor informed him that research was not a path to wealth. "There is more to life than money," Jonas replied. He was accepted to New York University's medical school.

It was while he was still a medical student that Jonas became interested in vaccines. At the time, vaccines were available for some viruses, such as smallpox. These vaccines used a weakened version of the virus to induce a mild infection that would produce antibodies and leave the patient immune to a dangerous illness. Jonas wanted to know if it was possible for a killed virus to do the same. In his last year of medicine, he succeeded in using dead influenza virus to make lab mice immune to influenza. It was an important step in a career that would lead him to develop the first vaccine for polio.

In 1955, he succeeded. Overnight, he became a hero, and countries rushed to begin mass polio immunization campaigns using his vaccine. Today, this terrible disease has been nearly eradicated worldwide.

Jonas Salk never patented his vaccine—he wanted it to be used as widely as possible. He was more interested in saving lives than in making money. He believed that we would eventually develop ways to prevent most diseases. To help make that happen, he and his supporters established the Salk Institute for Biological Studies in California, where creative and passionate scientists can work. As he explained, "Hope lies in dreams, in imagination and in the courage of those who dare to make dreams into reality."

FLORENCE NIGHTINGALE

The Invention of Modern Nursing

A hundred years ago, nursing was seen as an unskilled job. Nurses were treated like servants and received little training. Today, thanks to Florence Nightingale, nurses are highly educated and respected healthcare professionals. As a child, she was already trying to save lives—of dogs and mice!

Florence's family was British, but her parents were living abroad when she and her sister were born. Florence was named for her birthplace: Florence, Italy. Her older sister was named Parthenope, after the Greek settlement that is now part of the Italian city of Naples. At home, the girls were often known as Parthe and Flo.

In 1821, the year after Flo was born, the family returned to England. Flo's father, William Edward Nightingale, known as WEN, and was from a wealthy family. He had a stately home built and named it Lea Hurst. Flo later described it as "a small house with only fifteen bedrooms." When she was about two, her family moved to an enormous mansion called Embley Park, in Hampshire. Lea Hurst continued to be their summer home. Many years later, Lea Hurst was turned into a nursing home, and Embley became a school.

Even with two large homes, it was rare for the family to be in one place for any length of time. They traveled a lot and often stayed in hotels in London for weeks at a time, or they visited their different sets of relatives. Wherever they were staying, Flo and Parthe were rarely alone. Their family had many servants, and the girls were closely supervised. If their mother, Fanny, was away, one of their aunts looked after them or they were sent to stay with other family members. They had a nurse and a governess. They even had servants to dress them and do their hair every morning.

Flo and Parthe were part of a large group of cousins, and they were in regular contact with many of them. When Flo was about seven, her cousin Henry stayed with the family at Embley. Flo taught Henry French, and he taught her Latin. They wrote GOOD and BAD on little cards and hung them around each other's necks. Flo had fun staying with her cousin Jack as well. The two of them built a playhouse together. Flo was nine, and she wrote to her sister Parthe about their adventures: "We have made a sofa in the kitchen, covered with heather. Our moss-beds are so wet we cannot sleep in them."

Flo was an enthusiastic letter writer and spoke both English and French fluently. In fact, when she was eight, she decided to write her own autobiography in French: *La vie de Florence Rossignol.* But while she loved words, she did not like having to practice her handwriting. She wrote in spiky printing, not the elegant cursive that girls were expected to use. Her governess, Miss Christie, made her work in a "copybook," writing phrases over and over again. Flo got partway through, but then she rebelled and wrote this instead: "Stupid Copybook . . . I do not like it, I never wish to write it and I never will if I can help it."

Flo's handwriting difficulties might have been related to a medical condition. As a child, her hands and ankles were weak, and until she was a teenager, she had to wear special steel-lined boots for support. That didn't stop her from exploring the countryside. She had a pony at Lea Hurst, and during the summers, she would ride around the hills and moors. Flo loved animals. Her other pets included a pig, a donkey, and many dogs, including two named Peppercorn and Teaser. She even made friend with a small bird called a nuthatch.

When Flo was twelve, one of the family's maids found a nest of newborn mice in a mattress. Flo did her best to save the tiny creatures, wrapping them up in a basket near the fire and dropping warm milk into their mouths. Several died, but one survived the night. "I think it is possible it may live, poor little thing!" she wrote to her mother. "I should like to rear one, only one, so much. It would be so interesting to watch it."

When a collie with a broken leg was found near her home at Embley, Flo saved him, too. The shepherd who owned the dog thought he should be put down, but Flo was sure the injury could be treated. She nursed the dog back to health, and Cap the collie went on to live for many more years, running around on his three good legs.

Flo also became interested in human sicknesses. In her letters and notebooks, she recorded the details of her family members' medical conditions, from her uncle's lumbago to the nurse's swollen leg. When Flo was nine, her cousin Thomas—whom she called Bonny—died after being ill for six months. She was very close to him, and during his illness, she sent him little gifts. She also gave him a complete list of all the books she owned, in case he wanted to borrow any of them.

During the Victorian times that Flo grew up in, children were supposed to be obedient and respectful, but Flo was a clever, energetic, observant child with an independent mind. She liked to question everything. To adults, she sometimes seemed cheeky—like the time she wrote to her aunt about an eclipse of the moon: "Papa says that you were blind boobies if you did not watch it for a whole hour as we did."

Her mother and Miss Christie tried hard to turn her into a compliant, dutiful, grateful child like her sister Parthe. Much later, Florence wrote that her governess "did not understand children, and she used to shut me up for six weeks at a time. My sister, on the contrary, she spoilt." Flo was aware that her own mother thought she needed improvement: "I do not eat too much, I assure you, and I do not play too much. I lie down sometimes," she assured her in one letter when she was ten years old.

Hee hee!

Luckily, Flo's life became easier around this time.
Her aunt Mai came to look after the household while
WEN and Fanny were away. Mai was fond of Flo and
would never have allowed her to be locked up for weeks.
By the time Flo turned ten, the strict Miss Christie had
left the Nightingales—first for a few months, to care for
her sick brother, and then permanently, when she
married.

So, Flo's teenage years were mostly happy ones. She
and her sister were close. Both girls loved art, music,
and books. When Flo was fourteen, she stayed for a
while on the south coast of England, helping her Aunt
Julia look after her young cousins. She wrote to her aunt
Mai, "I felt somewhat forlorn when Mama and Papa
departed and my room and my bed are too large without
Parthe." Even when they were apart, as they often were,

the sisters wrote affectionate letters to each other—and once, when Parthe was too slow to respond, Flo wrote, "Why don't you write? Naughty girl!...I shall not write to you if you don't write for me."

After Miss Christie's departure, Flo and Parthe's father took on the responsibility for his daughters' education. They studied hard—sometimes Florence got up at three in the morning to begin work! By age sixteen, she was learning chemistry, physics, geography, astronomy, and mathematics, as well as French and Italian. By nineteen, she was also studying German and had mastered Latin and Greek. It was the kind of education that an upper-class boy might have received, but at the time, it was very unusual for a girl. Wealthy young ladies were expected to marry. They were not supposed to study or have careers.

But Florence didn't want to lead the kind of life expected of girls of her social class. She was intelligent and curious, and she had a strong desire to help others. By age fifteen, she was visiting people in the village, delivering blankets and food and caring for the sick. She met a local doctor, who gave her advice about nursing and medicine. A year later, when a flu epidemic hit the area, Florence rose to the occasion. She enjoyed all "the agitation and hurry" of the work. "At all events," she wrote a month later, "I have killed no patients, though I have cured few."

In her early twenties, she decided to pursue nursing. Her family objected, but Florence could not be deterred. A decade later, during the Crimean War, she traveled to Turkey with a team of volunteer nurses to care for injured British soldiers. She soon discovered that many more soldiers were dying of infectious diseases than from their wounds, and she thought the dirty, overcrowded conditions were to blame. The male doctors were not happy to have nurses in a military hospital, but Florence persisted. By applying scientific principles and working to improve hygiene, she succeeded in dramatically reducing the death rate.

By the time Florence Nightingale returned to England, she was well-known. She used her reputation to transform nursing in her own country. She started a nursing school in London, the first of its kind, and worked to improve healthcare for all, especially people living in poverty. International Nurses Day is celebrated on her birthday each year.

FOUR

TRAILBLAZERS

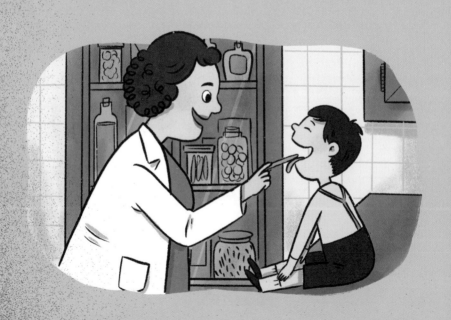

★ ★ FROM ★ ★

EDUCATION

TO

ANIMATION,

★ THESE ★

DETERMINED

AND CREATIVE

KID INNOVATORS

DEFIED THE ODDS,

DID THE UNEXPECTED,

★ AND ★

BROKE NEW GROUND.

MARIA MONTESSORI

Rethinking Education

Maria Montessori developed a ground-breaking new approach to educating children. Her revolutionary ideas about learning are an important part of today's education system—but the schools she attended as a child were the opposite of the ones that carry her name.

Maria was born in Chiaravalle, Ancona, at a time of great change. After a series of revolutions and wars of independence, the different states of the Italian peninsula became unified as the Kingdom of Italy, with Rome as the capital, in 1871—the year after Maria was born.

Maria's family was relatively wealthy. Her father, Allesandro Montessori, was an accountant and a traditional military man. Her mother, Renilde Stoppani, was the niece of Antonio Stoppani, a famous Italian geologist and paleontologist. Renilde was unusually well-educated for a woman at that time, and she was more progressive and open to change than her conservative husband. Once, when Maria was small, she heard her parents arguing. She pulled up a chair between them, climbed up on it, and joined her parents' hands together. She was always a peacemaker.

Because of her father's work, the family moved to an apartment in Rome when Maria was five years old. Rome was the capital and had a university, libraries, museums, and theaters. Artists and writers and students filled the streets and cafés. There was so much for Maria to do and see.

Maria started elementary school at age six. At this time, education in Italy was not very good. It wasn't until she was seven that the law required children to attend school, and even after this new law was passed, it was not enforced. In factories, mines, and fields, child labor was common. There was a big gap between rich and poor, and many children needed to work to help support their families. The majority of the country's population could not read or write.

The people making decisions about schools were often poorly educated. Teachers were untrained, badly paid, and given little respect. Many schools were overcrowded and dirty, and classrooms lacked books and even ink or pens. In these difficult circumstances, teachers did little to encourage a love of learning or to foster children's imaginations. Instead, classrooms were a place for endless memorization and drilling.

In smaller towns, schools taught only the basics of literacy and numeracy. But at Maria's school in Rome, history and geography were taught, as well as basic science. Although she was lucky to have a more well-

rounded education than many children at the time, Maria was not very interested or ambitious when she was young. Once, when she found another child crying about failing a grade and not moving up to the next class, Maria was puzzled; it seemed to her that one classroom was just as good as another. Her early school record was not particularly impressive, though she did earn a certificate for good behavior in first grade. The next year, she was given an award for *lavori donneschi*, or "women's work"—sewing and needlework.

Maria was a confident and strong-willed child. When playing games, she was usually the leader, but at times her innate confidence and assertiveness led her to be rather bossy. Although she was generally seen as a sweet child, she could also be impatient and even a little rude. She once said to a classmate, "Please remind me that I have made up my mind never to speak to you again." If a friend annoyed her, she didn't hesitate to express her disapproval. "You! Why, you are not even born yet," she would say dismissively. Some kids went home and complained to their parents about Maria's comments.

After school, Maria was expected to help her neighbors, especially those who were poor. She had to do a set amount of knitting every day to make warm items for those who needed them. She also gave herself tasks: when it was time to clean the floor, she would assign herself a certain number of squares to wash. She enjoyed this structure and found it very satisfying.

Years later, as an educator, Maria emphasized the importance of respect for children. Perhaps she remembered being treated without much respect by some of her own teachers. According to those who knew her, she had a strong sense of personal dignity as a child. Once, a teacher made a critical remark about the expression in Maria's eyes—after that, Maria never looked up at that teacher again.

When Maria was ten, she was very sick. Her mother worried, but Maria reassured her. "Do not worry, Mother," she said. "I cannot die; I have too much to do." She thought she might like to be an actress. But as she got older, she began doing well at school and realized that she excelled at learning. She took her studies more seriously and became interested in mathematics. One time, she even took her math book to the theater and studied during the performance!

After grade three, boys and girls were taught separately. The schools for girls didn't focus on math and science—the subjects that most interested Maria— so when she was twelve, she decided to attend an all-boys technical school. Her mother was encouraging, sitting up late with Maria and talking about her plans. Her father, being more traditional, was not as pleased with his daughter's unconventional choices, but Maria and her mother persisted. That fall, having just turned thirteen, Maria began school at the Regia Scuola Tecnica Michelangelo Buonarroti. The few girls who attended were not allowed to spend time with the boys, so at recess they stayed in a room on their own.

This new school taught a wider range of subjects but was no more imaginative in its approach than her old school. Students had to sit still, listen to lectures, and remember the facts they were taught. Everyone worked at the same pace, regardless of their interests or abilities. There was no questioning, discussion of ideas, critical thinking, or room for independence. Kids were expected to absorb the information their teachers delivered and repeat it exactly as taught.

Maria's parents suggested that she could become a teacher one day. At the time, teaching was one of the few careers available to women, who were expected only to marry and have children. But Maria refused to even consider it. She wanted to be an engineer, she told them. That was a bold idea for a girl at this time. Maria must have had a strong will and independent mind to come through the Italian school system and emerge as such an original, creative, and critical thinker.

In 1886, at fifteen years old, Maria graduated from the technical school with excellent marks in everything except drawing. She then continued her studies at a technical institute named for Leonardo da Vinci, spending the next four years focusing on modern languages, science, and math. By the time she was ready to graduate, she had abandoned the idea of engineering and picked a profession even more unlikely for a girl— medicine! She found biology fascinating, but no woman in Italy had ever become a doctor, and her father did not approve at all. Maria made an appointment to meet with a professor at the University of Rome's medical school. They had a friendly conversation, but he told her that a future in medicine would be impossible. When leaving, Maria shook his hand and told him, "I know I shall become a doctor."

Despite being treated badly by male students and professors, Maria graduated with a degree in medicine at the age of twenty-six, making her the first woman in Italy to become a doctor. After graduating, she began a private medical practice and worked mostly with children with disabilities. At this time, there were few opportunities for children with disabilities to attend school, but Maria believed that all children were capable of learning.

Maria became increasingly interested in education, studying different approaches and developing her own ideas. She believed that all children should be recognized as individuals and that independence, not obedience and memorization, should be the goal of education. Children had a natural desire to learn, she said, and they needed an environment that supported them in discovery and growth. Her approach, known as the Montessori Method, is used in about twenty thousand Montessori Schools around the world, and her ideas have influenced millions of teachers worldwide.

A more recent innovator in the field of education is the American mathematician **Salman Khan**. Salman didn't start out as a teacher, but he had degrees in math and computer science, so when his twelve-year-old cousin Nadia needed help with math, he began tutoring her online. When relatives and friends heard about Nadia's improved skills, they wanted Salman's tutoring as well. To save time and make scheduling easier, Salman started recording his tutorials and sharing them on YouTube. The videos were soon so popular that he quit his full-time job to focus on developing Khan Academy, a nonprofit educational organization that provides free education to anyone, anywhere. His videos are available in numerous languages and have been viewed more than 1.6 billion times; they are used in homes and schools in many different countries. In 2012, *Time* magazine named Salman Khan one of the 100 most influential people in the world.

MADAM C. J. WALKER

Craving the Beautiful

Madam C. J. Walker invented a line of hair and beauty products for black women and founded the Madam C. J. Walker Manufacturing Company. She was one of the first American women to become a self-made millionaire—but first she had to overcome great loss, poverty, and hardship.

Her real name was Sarah Breedlove, and she was born near Delta, Louisiana, two days before Christmas in 1867. Her great-great-granddaughter later wrote that Sarah's birth must have been a symbol of hope for her family: She was their first child to be born free. Sarah's parents, Minerva and Owen, had been enslaved, and her four older siblings were born into slavery.

Sarah's parents and siblings had worked on a plantation belonging to a white man named Robert W. Burney. Their labor, and the unpaid work of dozens of other enslaved people, helped build the estate and make its owner rich. After the Confederate army was defeated in the Civil War, much of Burney's property was destroyed. The Union army turned the land into a refugee camp where thousands of newly freed people struggled to survive in terrible conditions.

When Sarah was born, her family still lived on the same land, but little was left of the farm they had helped to build. Their home was a rickety cypress cabin near the banks of the Mississippi River. Spring rains led to floods and gnats, and mosquitoes swarmed around the people working in the humid cotton fields.

The Southern economic system had been built on the enslavement of African Americans, and although the Emancipation Proclamation ended slavery five years before Sarah's birth, racism and poverty continued. There was a great deal of political turmoil in those years, but Sarah's parents did their best to protect their children. Thanks to a successful cotton harvest, the family's financial situation was improving, and by the time Sarah was two, her parents were able to formally marry. They'd been together for over twenty years.

Sarah had four older brothers and sisters, ranging in age from seven to fifteen, and a new baby brother named Solomon.

Sarah's best friend was a girl named Celeste. The two children went to picnics and fish frys together, sat together at church, and even wore their hair in matching hairstyles. They played outside when they could and liked catching crawfish in the bayous. But they had to work hard, even at a young age, helping their parents in the cotton fields. Sarah and Celeste were competitive and took pride in how fast they worked.

Sarah was an intelligent child, but there were few public schools in Louisiana, and many white people were opposed to the idea of educating black children. They didn't want them to be in a classroom during harvest time, when workers were needed—and perhaps more important, they feared that education might make black people more likely to challenge the racist system. As a result, Sarah had only a few months of formal education. She was able to learn the alphabet and basic literacy at her church's Sunday school.

When Sarah was about five years old, her mother died. Her father remarried, but then he, too, died only a year later. Her parents' deaths were probably the result of infectious illnesses such as smallpox, cholera, or typhoid. These diseases were common at the time; there were no vaccinations to prevent them, and no effective treatment for people who became sick. "I had little or no opportunity when I started out in life," Sarah later recalled, "having been left an orphan and being without mother or father since I was seven years of age."

Sarah went to live with her older sister Louvenia. Louvenia's husband, Jesse, was cruel and had a violent temper, so life was not easy for Sarah. Failing crops and a yellow fever epidemic added to the stress. So did racism. Violence against black people in neighboring areas was increasing, and when Sarah was ten, she, Louvenia, and Jesse moved off the farm and into the nearby town of Vicksburg, on the other side of the river. One benefit of this move was that Sarah could see her older brother Alexander. He had been living in Vicksburg for a year and worked as a porter at the grocery store.

With no education, Louvenia and Jesse had trouble finding jobs. Sarah was expected to help the family by earning money. She found work doing laundry for the wealthy white families who lived in the town's mansions.

Sarah always loved luxurious things. She looked at expensive fabrics and hats and shoes in store windows and admired the fancy clothes of steamboat passengers who stopped in town. A reporter who interviewed her many years later wrote that, "as a child, she craved for the beautiful."

But it must have seemed unlikely to Sarah that she could ever afford such luxuries. The situation in Louisiana was worsening. Violence against black people was common, and it was almost impossible to earn a living. Many black people were fleeing north, searching for better opportunities. By the time Sarah was fourteen, her brothers had moved to St Louis, Missouri. Sarah knew that she, too, had to get away, but she had few options—so she ran away with a man named Moses McWilliams. It was a practical decision, not a romantic one. Later, she explained: "I married at the age of fourteen in order to get a home of my own." Three years later, Sarah had a baby and named her Leila. When Leila was just a toddler, Moses died, leaving Sarah to raise the child alone. So, she headed north to St. Louis, where her brothers were working as barbers.

After living in Delta and Vicksburg, St. Louis must have seemed like a big city to Sarah. It had department stores and insurance companies, paved boulevards, and a huge train station. It was home to the world's largest brewery and the world's largest manufacturer of chewing tobacco. Sarah rented a room in a cheap part of town, living on a street that was well-known to the police for violent crimes. She needed to find a way to support herself and her daughter—and again, she found no alternative but to do laundry. It was hard work and didn't pay much. Sometimes she worked as a cook as well. But no matter how hard she worked, she earned no more than about $1.50 a day. For the next ten years, she and Leila struggled to keep a roof over their heads.

But Sarah had big dreams. She wanted a better life, and she was determined that her daughter would have a

brighter future. By the time Leila was seventeen, Sarah had managed to save enough to send her to boarding school. Then, Sarah began taking night classes and volunteering in the community, and in 1904, she got a job selling hair-care products. It was something she knew a lot about: from her brothers, who were barbers, but also from personal experience. Years earlier, Sarah's hair had begun to fall out. She experimented with different concoctions, trying to find something that would help. Now, with her previous knowledge and her new experience in sales, she moved to Denver, Colorado, and began selling her own line of hair-care products.

Sarah also began a relationship with a man named Charles Joseph (C. J.) Walker. Like Sarah, he was smart and ambitious. He was someone she could imagine a future with. Charles became her business partner and gave her advice on how to advertise and promote her products. Soon, she was traveling around the country giving demonstrations. She eventually started a factory to make cosmetics and opened a hair salon and beauty school to train her sales agents. She employed thousands of people and helped many other black women start their own businesses and become financially independent.

Sarah was also a great philanthropist, giving away money to help her community. She funded scholarships, supported the arts, assisted schools and orphanages, and donated funds to fight racism. In 1912, in her mid-forties, she spoke to the National Negro Business League, saying, "I am a woman who came from the cotton fields of the South. From there, I was promoted to the washtub. From there, I was promoted to the cook kitchen. And from there, I promoted myself into the business of manufacturing hair goods and preparations. I have built my own factory on my own ground."

WALT DISNEY

Creating Happiness

When you hear the name Walt Disney, you probably think of theme parks and animated films, Mickey Mouse and Disney princesses. But long before he became an artist and entrepreneur, Walt Disney was just a kid drawing horses on a farm in Missouri.

Walt was born on Chicago's West Side in 1901. He had three older brothers—Herbert, Raymond, and Roy—and a younger sister, Ruth. When he was four years old, his parents, Elias and Flora, sold their house and moved to a farm just outside Marceline, Missouri.

The day the family arrived at the farm was one of Walt's earliest memories. "My first impression of it was that it had a beautiful front yard with lots of weeping willow trees," he recalled. "We had every kind of an apple growing in that orchard." They also had chickens, cows, horses, and hogs—on whose backs Walt sometimes rode. Walt's brother Roy said the farm was heaven for city kids.

The town of Marceline, with its shop-lined avenue, held great appeal for young Walt. In 1908, the town had only two automobiles. But it had trains—and Walt was a big fan of trains.

Elias was strict and often quick-tempered with his children, but Walt loved him very much. He described his father as "the kindest fellow." Flora was a loving mother with a sense of humor, and she found ways of working around her husband's rules. When money was tight, Elias didn't want the kids eating butter that he could have sold, so she would put butter on the underside of their bread. "Look, there's no butter on the bread," the kids would say to their dad while eating bread that was thickly buttered underneath!

Walt didn't start school until he was eight years old, so he had plenty of time for fun during those years on the farm. He started drawing, and some of his elderly neighbors and relatives gave him paper and crayons. "One of my fondest childhood memories is of Doc

Sherwood," Walt recalled. "He used to encourage me in my drawing and gave me little presents for my efforts. One time, I think he must have held a horse of his nearly all day so that I could draw it. Needless to say, the drawing wasn't so hot, but Doc made me think it was tops." Once, Walt drew animals on the side of the house, using soft tar. "I wasn't thanked for my efforts by the family," he admitted.

Later in life, Walt always thought of Marceline as his childhood home—Main Street, U.S.A. in the Disney theme parks was inspired by the town—but he lived on the farm for only four years. When Walt was nearly nine, his father became ill, prompting his parents to sell the property and move to Kansas City. The next few years were much tougher for Walt. He started a new school and had to repeat second grade. From his

ıs catapulted into years of

a newspaper delivery

ears, Walt delivered papers

. He got up at 4:30 a.m. and

school. Exhausted, he often

l, but Walt was expected to

mily. So, he tried other ways

When he was ten, he opened a

ut three weeks. "We drank up all

confessed.

alt was fifteen, his parents and Ruth moved

vhere Elias was manager for a jelly

alt stayed behind, living with two of his

s. By lying about his age and pretending to

e got a job selling candy, fruit, and drinks

on the trains. Unfortunate

make matters worse, he co

By the end of the summer, h

employer. Still, he loved ridin

That fall, Walt joined his

sixteen, he started grade eigh

School, washed bottles, and cr

factory. He also started taking

his cartoons in the school news

thought they were special. He love

laugh, though; he put on plays at schoo

with his friend Walter Pfeiffer, whose moth

accompanied them on the piano. Walter and

introduced Walt to vaudeville and motion p

This was Walt's last year of school. It wa

the United States was fighting at war. Walt

Roy had joined the Navy, and Walt wanted to sign up as well, but he was too young. So, he forged his birth date to appear older and joined the Red Cross as an ambulance driver. It was the year of the devastating flu epidemic, and before Walt was sent to France, he fell sick. By the time he recovered, the war had ended. Walt spent nearly a year in France anyway. He drew cartoons for the canteen menu, on the canvas flaps of his ambulance, and for the army newspaper, as well as caricatures for friends to send back home.

By the time he returned to Chicago, Walt knew he wanted to work in the arts. He moved back to Kansas City and at eighteen, he began working as an illustrator. He studied animation and started a business making short cartoons.

At twenty-one, Walt moved to Hollywood. "I arrived here in August 1923 with $30 in my pocket," he said. "One half of my suitcase had my shirts and underwear . . . the other half had my drawing materials." He and Roy started the Disney Brothers Studio, which went on to become the Walt Disney Company. Walt hired an artist named Lillian Bounds, whom he later married. She persuaded him to name his mouse character Mickey!

Walt Disney became an artist and entrepreneur, a pioneer in animation, and a movie producer who has won more Academy Awards than anyone else. He was a visionary, moving beyond the world of film to create the first Disney theme park, Disneyland. Today, the Walt Disney Company earns billions of dollars every year. But for Walt, success was about more than money: it was about pursuing his dreams, making people laugh, bringing families together . . . and creating happiness.

Long before movies existed, innovators found ways to make animated—or moving—images, creating devices that were sold as toys. The first to become popular was called the phénakistiscope, which was invented by **Joseph Plateau** in 1833. It was made of a spinning disk attached to a handle. Around the disk's center were a series of drawings and a series of equally spaced cut-out slits. The user spun the disk and looked through the moving slits at the disk's reflection in a mirror, which appeared to be a moving picture. It must have seemed like magic. Even today, film students study these early devices because they help demonstrate the basic principles of animation.

ALVIN AILEY

All That Was Inside You

Alvin Ailey was one of the greatest innovators in the world of modern dance, but as a child, he had no idea that he would become a dancer one day. It wasn't until he was in his late teens that he learned that a career in dance was even possible for a man.

Alvin was born into a full house in the Brazos Valley of Texas in 1931. His grandfather shared the home with Alvin's mother, his aunt and uncle, and eight cousins. The doctor said that little Alvin was one of the most alert and curious babies he had ever seen.

Alvin was named after his father, Alvin Senior, who had left when his son was still an infant. Little Alvin moved around with his mother, Lula, as she looked for work to support them. His earliest memories were of searching for somewhere to belong—walking from place to place, staying with relatives, and renting a house with no furniture in Rogers, Texas. In the front yard was a big tree full of praying mantises. Alvin called them Devil's horses, and he was terrified of them. One day, he shook the tree and thousands of the insects rained down around him!

Alvin grew up during the Great Depression, in the American South, where racial segregation and discrimination were legal. In his town, there was a black school at the bottom of the hill; it was poor and rundown. The white children went to a school at the top of the hill, which to Alvin looked like a castle. "Texas was a tough place for a black boy in the 1930s," he recalled.

At age four or five, Alvin worked alongside his mother, picking cotton under the hot sun. When he got tired, he'd wander off and look for snakes on the road.

Alvin's mother was often away working, but he knew that she loved him very much. They would take walks together in the woods, and Alvin used to pick wildflowers for her. One time, when he became sick after eating half-cooked beans, Lula carried him on her back for eight miles to find a doctor.

When Alvin was about eight, he and his mother moved to live with a man named Amos Alexander, whom Alvin described as "a wonderful, tall black man who had a big limp." Amos was kind to Alvin; he gave him a dog, taught him to ride horses, and showed him how to plant fruit trees. Alvin felt as if he finally had a home. He didn't even mind doing chores—feeding the chickens, looking after the cows and hogs, working in the garden. Best of all, Amos had a record player and an old piano. "Thus, for many hours I could lose myself in the music that had always enthralled me," Alvin recalled.

But it was during this happy time that something frightening happened. Behind the house was a big water tank. It was twenty feet deep, with slippery edges. Alvin had been warned to stay away from it, but during the hot summers, he and his friend used to play nearby to cool off. One day, Alvin fell in. He couldn't swim and thrashed around desperately—then he slipped beneath the surface. Luckily, his friend managed to pull him out, saving him from drowning.

Despite the racism and poverty that surrounded him, Alvin remembered his years in Texas as "a time of love, a time of caring, a time when people didn't have much but they had each other." In particular, church made a huge impression on him. Some of the things he saw—a procession of people dressed all in white walking to the lake to be baptized, women in the pews singing and fluttering their fans—later made their way into the ballets he choreographed.

Alvin never knew his biological father, and this absence greatly affected him. He felt as though he was the only kid without a dad. Amos was the first man he felt that he could call a father, but when Alvin was twelve, his mother decided to leave Amos and move to Los Angeles.

It was 1942, and Los Angeles was booming. Although Alvin hadn't wanted to leave Texas, he found it exciting to live in a big city. He attended George Washington Carver Junior High School. He lived close by, so his friends would come to his house for lunch, and every Friday they would go to the movies at a nearby theater named after the dancer Bill Robinson. Alvin also discovered the Lincoln, a vaudeville theater that featured films and live shows. For only fifty cents admission, Alvin saw chorus lines, dancers, and entertainers of all kinds, including the great jazz musician Duke Ellington, perform there. The theater had a big influence on him, and he later said that he was "bowled over by the glitter and the glitz."

One of Alvin's teachers introduced him to choral music, and he fell in love with Gilbert and Sullivan's *Mikado*. As soon as the teacher left the room, Alvin would get up and sing the opera's music. Then he discovered the movies of Gene Kelly and Fred Astaire. Watching the actors dance moved him deeply: "The idea came to me that moving around could express all that was inside you." In his backyard, Alvin copied their steps and began making up his own. Tap dancing was popular in his neighborhood, and Alvin decided to try it. His mom bought him tap shoes, but he went to only three lessons. "It just wasn't me," he said.

When Alvin started high school, he had no intention of becoming a dancer. He'd been raised in a world that taught him that men didn't dance and that boys who danced were "sissy." "You couldn't even *think* about dancing," he recalled. His gym teacher pushed him to play football, but he hated it and lasted only two weeks. He tried track but didn't like that either. "I felt defeated by my total failure at competitive sports," he later said.

Finally, Alvin discovered gymnastics, which reminded him of the dancing he'd been doing in his yard. When one of his teachers took the class to a ballet at the Philharmonic Auditorium, Alvin was amazed by the sight and sounds of the fifty-piece orchestra. Soon, he began spending time in the theater district and going to musicals. And then the Katherine Dunham Company came to town. It was led by a black woman, with a group of black male dancers. "They were superb," Alvin recalled. "I was lifted up into another realm. I couldn't believe there were black people on a legitimate stage in downtown Los Angeles." He hung around the stage doors every day, until one of the dancers noticed and arranged for him to be allowed in when the seats weren't full. He saw the show eight times!

Despite his enthusiasm, Alvin still wasn't considering a career in dance. He thought he might be a preacher—after all, it was a kind of performance to dress up and stand before a congregation, holding them spellbound. Or perhaps he could become a writer or a language teacher. He wrote poetry, and his Spanish was so good that his high school teacher sometimes let him lead the class.

Then one day, at a school assembly, Alvin saw a student named Carmen de Lavallade dancing to Mozart. He was fascinated and began waiting in the halls outside her classes. Eventually, they became close friends. When Carmen saw Alvin doing gymnastics, she invited him to watch her dance class at the studio of a man named Lester Horton. Alvin agreed, and he was thrilled by what he saw. The studio was in Hollywood— a ninety-minute bus ride away—but for the next month,

Alvin went with Carmen, three times a week, just to watch. Soon, Lester invited him to join the class, and then to rehearse with Carmen. "Dance, for me, would have been impossible without Carmen de Lavallade," he later said.

Alvin continued studying with Lester, and by the time he was twenty-two, he had decided to be a dancer. He knew he would have to forge his own path. At the time, there were few opportunities for black people in the world of dance, and as a gay black man, Alvin faced homophobia as well as racism. Nevertheless, only five years after he dedicated himself to dance, he founded one of the world's most successful dance companies: the Alvin Ailey American Dance Theater.

Blending theater with modern dance, ballet, and jazz, and centering African American experiences and musical traditions, Alvin Ailey created many ballets, including his famous *Revelations*, one of the most popular ballets of all time. His legacy continues today. The Alvin Ailey Dance Theater still trains young dancers, and the company has performed ballets for more than twenty-five million people across the United States and in more than seventy countries around the world.

Further Reading

Bibliography

There are many great books about great innovators, including autobiographies (books written by the person about their own life) and biographies (books about noteworthy people written by someone else). The following is a list of the main sources used by the author in researching and writing this book.

General Interest

Quirky: The Remarkable Story of the Traits, Foibles, and Genius of Breakthrough Innovators Who Changed the World, by Melissa A. Schilling. Hachette, 2018.

PART ONE

Grace Hopper

Grace Hopper: Admiral of the Cyber Sea, by Kathleen Broome Williams. Naval Institute Press 2012.

Grace Hopper and the Invention of the Information Age, by Kurt W. Beyer. The MIT Press, 2012.

Steve Jobs

Steve Jobs: The Man Who Thought Different: A Biography, by Karen Blumenthal. Square Fish, 2012.

Steve Jobs, by Walter Isaacson. Simon & Schuster, 2011.

"Steve Jobs Interview: One-on-One in 1995." https://www.pcworld.com/article/241370/steve_jobs_interview_oneonone_in_1995.html

Bill Gates

Gates: How Microsoft's Mogul Reinvented an Industry and Made Himself the Richest Man in America, by Stephen Manes and Paul Andrews. Cadwallader & Stern, 2013.

Inside Bill's Brain: Decoding Bill Gates. Documentary. Directed by Davis Guggenheim. 2019.

Reshma Saujani

Reshma Saujani: Girls Who Code Founder, by Jill Sherman. Lerner, 2018.

Women Who Don't Wait in Line: Break the Mold, Lead the Way, by Reshma Saujani. Amazon, 2013.

"Not Everyone Can Afford a Job They Love: Why the Founder of Girls Who Code Stayed in a Role She Hated Before Leaving the Private Sector," by Lola Fadulu. *The Atlantic,* July 17, 2018. https://www.theatlantic.com/technology/archive/2018/07/reshma-saujani-girls-who-code/562055

"RESHMA: How a Daughter of Refugees Taught Girls to Code, Won over Tech Millionaires, and Pushed Her Way into Politics," by Alyson Shontell. *Business Insider,* August 23, 2013. https://www.businessinsider.com/reshma-saujani-profile-2013-8

"Why Can't I Be You: Reshma Saujani," by Amber Humphrey. *Rookie,* January 25, 2016. https://www.rookiemag.com/2016/01/reshma-saujani-girls-who-code

PART TWO

Jacques Cousteau

Jacques Cousteau: The Sea King, by Brad Matsen. New York: Random House. 2009.

My Father, the Captain: My Life with Jacques Cousteau, by Jean-Michel Cousteau, Daniel Paisner. National Geographic, 2010.

Wilbur and Orville Wright

The Wright Brothers, by David McCullough. Simon & Schuster, 2015.

William Kamkwamba

The Boy Who Harnessed the Wind, by William Kamkwamba. William Morrow, 2009.

Elon Musk

Elon Musk: Tesla, SpaceX, and the Quest for a Fantastic Future, by Ashlee Vance. Harper Collins, 2015.

PART THREE

Alan Turing

Alan Turing: The Enigma, by Andrew Hodges. Vintage, 2012.

Alan M. Turing, by Sara Turing. Cambridge University Press, 2012.

Hedy Lamarr

Hedy's Folly: The Life and Breakthrough Inventions of Hedy Lamarr, the Most Beautiful Woman in the World, by Richard Rhodes. Vintage, 2011.

Beautiful: The Life of Hedy Lamarr, by Stephen Michael Shearer. Thomas Dunne Books, 2010.

Jonas Salk

Jonas Salk, by Charlotte DeCroes Jacobs. Oxford University Press, 2015.

Polio: An American Story, by David M. Oshinsky. Oxford University Press, 2005.

Florence Nightingale

Florence Nightingale: The Woman and her Legend, by Mark Bostridge. Penguin, 2008.

Nightingales: The Extraordinary Upbringing and Curious Life of Miss Florence Nightingale, by Gillian Gill. Random House, 2004.

PART FOUR

Madam C. J. Walker

On Her Own Ground: The Life and Times of Madam C. J. Walker, by A'Leila Bundles. Simon and Schuster, 2001.

Walt Disney

"The Marceline I Knew," by Walt Disney. *Marcelline News*, September 2, 1938. https://www.dix-project.net/item/2689/marceline-news-the-marceline-i-knew

The Animated Man: A Life of Walt Disney, by Michael Barrier. University of California Press, 2007.

Maria Montessori

Maria Montessori: A Biography, by Rita Kramer. Diversion Books, 2017.

Maria Montessori: Her Life and Work, by E. M. Standing. Penguin, 1998.

Alvin Ailey

Revelations: The Autobiography of Alvin Ailey, with A. Peter Bailey. Citadel Press, 1995.

Index

V

vaccines and vaccination, 139, 169
violence against black people,
   169–70

W

Walker, Madam C. J. (Sarah
   Breedlove), 165–74
windmill, 92, 93
wireless networks, 127
World War I, 24, 62, 120, 180–81
World War II, 69, 116, 118
World Wide Web, 57
Wright Flyer I, 80
Wright, Wilbur and Orville, 11,
   71–81

Y

YouTube, 164

They're Little Kids with Big Dreams . . . and Big Problems!

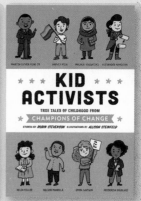